ONE DAY
AT A TIME
IN
AL-ANON

Other Al-Anon Books:

Al-Anon Faces Alcoholism

Living with an Alcoholic

The Dilemma of the Alcoholic Marriage

Al-Anon's Favorite Forum Editorials

Alateen—Hope for Children of Alcoholics

ONE DAY
AT A TIME
IN
AL-ANON

Al-Anon Family Group
Headquarters, Inc.
NEW YORK
1978

© Al-Anon Family Group Headquarters, Inc. 1973
Post Office Box 182
Madison Square Station
New York, New York 10010

Twelfth Printing November 1978
Library of Congress Card No. 72—85153
ISBN—0—910034—21—4

Approved by
World Service Conference
Al-Anon Family Groups

Printed and Bound
by T.H. Best Printing Company Limited,
Don Mills, Canada

This book suggests living one day at a time, and the ways in which we may find in each day a measure of comfort, serenity and a sense of achievement.

It discourages dwelling on past errors and disappointments; visualizes the future only as a series of new days, each a fresh opportunity for self-realization and growth.

Today is only a small manageable segment of time in which our difficulties need not overwhelm us. This lifts from our hearts and minds the heavy weight of both past and future.

* * *

Although we generally refer to the Al-Anon member as "she," there are men as well as women in most Al-Anon groups.

* * *

Mindful of the fact that the Al-Anon fellowship embraces people of many lands, creeds and customs, the book avoids, so far as possible, identification with those of the United States where Al-Anon happened to have had its beginning. These daily messages are intended for all people, all ways of life.

QUOTATIONS

On most of these pages the message is reinforced by an appropriate quotation.

Those from copyrighted books are identified by title, author and publisher on page 367, for the convenience of those who wish to refer to the sources.

Quotations from the Scriptures of the Judeo-Christian faiths are identified by Book.

All unidentified quotations are by members of the Al-Anon fellowship and are therefore anonymous.

INDEX

An alphabetical index of the subjects covered in this book begins on page 368.

The Steps, Traditions,
Slogans and Serenity
Prayer may be found
at the end of the index.

This year is a book of clean blank pages on which I will write a record of my experiences and my growth through the daily use of the Al-Anon idea. I turned to Al-Anon as a last resort because I was living with a problem that was too much for me. I know I can deal with this problem through applying Al-Anon to myself, to my thoughts and my actions, every day. If I allow myself to be influenced by what the alcoholic says and does, it will make blots and smears on the pages of my year. This I will try to avoid at all costs.

Today's Reminder

I can live my life only one day at a time. Perhaps my confusion and despair are so great that I will have to take it one hour at a time, or one minute at a time, reminding myself constantly that I have authority over no life but my own.

"Realizing that nothing can hurt me while I lean upon my Higher Power, I ask to be guided through the hours and minutes of each day. Let me remind myself to bring every problem to Him for I know He will show me the way I must go."

If I were to sit down in a quiet corner and look back over the happenings of my troubled life *as though I were examining the life of someone else,* or reading about it in a book, how would it appear to me? I know I can do this only by guarding against all self-justification; looking at the facts honestly. Have I said or done things in haste, anger or desperation that made my situation worse? Are there things I recall with regret? We learn only from experience, and only by making up our minds not to repeat past mistakes.

Today's Reminder

I will not fall in with the alcoholic's craving for punishment to relieve his guilt. I will not scold and weep, for it will not help me overcome the difficulties we are trapped in. I will try very hard to deal with my day by day difficulties with quiet poise, remembering always that I am doing this for my own benefit.

"When I am tempted or pressured into irrational behavior, I pray that I may stop and think before I do or say anything whatever. I ask God to remove these impulses and help me to grow into the person I want to be."

Why do I waste my precious time and energy trying to figure out what makes an alcoholic drink—why he doesn't consider his family, his obligations, his reputation? All I need to know is that he suffers from a disease—alcoholism, the compulsion to drink. Why shouldn't I have compassion for him and his illness when I am so ready to feel sorry for people who have other diseases? Do I blame *them*? Why do I blame *him*? Can I cure him by reproaching him? Can I look into his heart and realize the true nature of his sufferings?

Today's Reminder

The fact that I am the spouse, child, parent, or friend of an alcoholic does not give me the right to try to control him. I can only make the situation worse by treating him like an irresponsible naughty child.

"On this day I promise God and myself that I will let go of the problem which is destroying my peace of mind. I pray for detachment from the situation, but not from the suffering drinker who may be helped to find the way to sobriety through the change in my attitude and the love and compassion I am able to express."

If I say "Of myself I can do nothing," I am asserting that I intend to seek help. Where is the help for my problem of living with an alcoholic? I will find it with my fellow-members in Al-Anon. There I will find understanding, strength and hope. There I will learn to accept the things I cannot change, the courage to change the things I can. My first step will be to have a program: I will go to every possible Al-Anon meeting, I will read Al-Anon literature, I will keep an open mind, I will apply what I learn to my everyday life.

Today's Reminder

My own way of thinking often deceives me. I can see but a little way. When I realize that people are learning to solve their problems in over 12,500 Al-Anon groups all over the world, wouldn't I be punishing myself needlessly to reject this wonderful way of life?

"Sharing experiences widens one's horizons and opens out new and better ways to deal with difficulties. There is no need to solve them alone."

This day I will concentrate on the inner meaning of the Commandment "Thou shalt love thy neighbor as thyself." I will accept myself, for that is the primary condition under which the good in me can grow. Unless I am at peace with the child of God I am, I cannot love and help my neighbor. Regrets are vain. They interfere with the good I could do today, the making of the better person I want to be tomorrow.

Today's Reminder

Condemning ourselves for mistakes we have made is just as bad as condemning others for theirs. We are not really equipped to make judgments, not even of ourselves.

Thomas A'Kempis said: "All perfection in this life is attended by some imperfection and all our farseeing is not without obscurity."

> "Today I pray for the wisdom to
> build a better tomorrow on the
> mistakes and experiences of
> yesterday."

Until I came into Al-Anon, I thought nobody had a problem as bad as mine. That gave me plenty of reason to feel sorry for myself, to resent what the alcoholic was doing, and to hammer away at his mistakes and short-comings.

As I attended Al-Anon meetings, my eyes began to open. Other people's problems made mine look small, yet they were facing them with courage and confidence. Others were trapped in situations as bad as mine, but they bore their troubles with more fortitude; they accepted the fact that the alcoholic was suffer-ing from a disease. I found many reasons to be grateful that my lot was not worse. My load began to lighten.

Today's Reminder

When things look blackest, it is within my power to brighten them with the light of under-standing and gratitude. I realize how much de-pends on my point of view; my own wrong habits of thinking and acting must be corrected and only I can do that.

> "Let me not expect easy solutions to my problems. Make me realize that many of my difficulties were created by me, by my own reactions to the happenings in my daily life. I ask only to be guided to a better way."

Someone said something unkind about me. Are my feelings hurt? Yes. Should they be? No. How do I overcome my hurt? By detaching myself, "turning it off," until I can figure out what lies behind it. If it was retaliation for an unkindness I did, let me correct my fault. If not, I have no responsibility in the matter. Should I ignore or challenge? No, I will let it go; least said, soonest mended. Nothing can hurt me unless I allow it to. When I am pained by anything that happens *outside* of myself, it is not *that thing* which hurts me, but the way I think and feel about it.

Today's Reminder

Let me not take to myself, and suffer over, the actions and reactions of other people. Other adult human beings are not my responsibility, no matter how closely their lives may be intertwined with mine. I will not allow myself to be troubled by anyone else; my one problem is to improve my own way of living and looking at life.

> "God teach me to detach my mind from what others say and do, except to draw helpful lessons and guidance from them."

When the alcoholic has been blessed with
the gift of sobriety, I can be grateful for the
many good consequences of the change: being
able to depend on his coming home on time so
the family can be together at the dinner table;
being able to invite friends in without fear of
embarrassment; having our bills paid so we
can hold our heads up.

If I am ever tempted to have misgivings
about this new-found sobriety, I will strive for
confidence; my trust will help him maintain
sobriety and keep me serene.

Today's Reminder

Even if there are many problems still to be
solved, I will make the most of the benefits that
sobriety brings. I will live the Al-Anon program
and depend on it to help me solve whatever problems are still to come.

> "I pray to learn to enjoy the good
> that each day brings and not to be
> apprehensive about the future,
> which is in God's hands."

When living with an alcoholic overwhelmed me, I didn't know which way to turn or how to make a decision. I rejected God because I resented what I considered unfair punishment. Yet I found that "going it alone" made matters even worse. At a still later stage of desperation, I turned to Him again and placed my life and my will in His hands. Once I had surrendered, trusting Him completely, my burdens were lightened. I cannot profess to understand how such things happen; I want never to forget that He is ready to befriend me, but only to the degree that I trust Him.

Today's Reminder

If instead of trusting in God I trust only my own intelligence, my own strength and my own prudence, I will not find my way to Him and His help. He has offered me the gift of faith. In accepting it, I must put aside my own human will and trust in Him. Dante, in the Divine Comedy, wrote: "In His will is our peace."

"Trust in the Lord with all thy heart
   and lean not unto thine own understanding.
   In all thy ways acknowledge Him and He
   shall direct thy paths."

(Proverbs)

We come to Al-Anon in order to share "experience, strength and hope with each other." Most of us, at first, come to "get"—not to give or share. What we want to *get* is sobriety for the alcoholic. We soon learn that this is beyond us. We are there to find serenity for ourselves, through giving and sharing.

Sometimes people who come to Al-Anon, desperate and helpless, partake of the healing interchange of the group, and then, after the alcoholics have found sobriety, feel they don't need Al-Anon any longer. Once over their own hurdle, they forget their obligation to help others.

Today's Reminder

Living with an alcoholic does not mean only a drinking alcoholic; it can also mean living with a person who is remaking his life so as to live without alcohol. If at any time we needed Al-Anon, the need does not vanish when sobriety comes into the picture.

It is by continuing to give of ourselves that we continue to receive. In helping others, we continue to enrich our own lives.

" 'Withhold not good from them to whom it
   is due when it is within the power of thy
   hand to do it,' says the Bible. I pray that I may
   not be tempted, by indifference or selfishness,
   to withhold from others the help I have
   received."

Once upon a time there was a woman who was very unhappy. If you asked her what she was unhappy about, she would say despairingly: "Oh, just everything! And then she would go into the most excruciating detail about her sufferings, the awful things her husband did, the trouble she had with her children. A scared, lugubrious expression was etched on her face. Although she had been a pretty girl, she could see no reason for making herself look nice—and anyway she didn't have the time. While she was looking on the dark side, communication and love between her and her family grew less and less. Even her friends avoided her, which increased her grievance against life. Everything would have been all right, of course, if only her husband would stop drinking, and she told him so every day.

Once in a while somebody would get her to an Al-Anon meeting, but somehow she had the idea that all the members were just waiting to hear her latest disaster reports.

One night a member, determined to help her if she could, put the cards on the table. She told her that everybody there had plenty of trouble, but with the help of Al-Anon and each other, they learned to stop exaggerating them. "Why don't you try wearing a smile for a change, and see what happens? Maybe it would even be such a jolt for your husband to see you pleasant and cheerful that he'd run to AA."

And, believe it or not, after a while that's just what happened!

Today I will examine my ideas of enjoyment, pleasure, delight. Have I grieved over the fact that my life has become empty of them? Do these satisfactions depend on parties, travel, dancing, movies, television? Do I feel deprived because I am busy with home, children, a job, so I am not free to pursue some recreation? If so, it is time I learned to enjoy the thousands of little things that occur in my daily life: a sunrise; the sound of birds; a long walk, noting all the interesting things I see; a piece of music; a good book; a charming response from a child; a moving story at an AA meeting; a small household chore perfectly performed; a beautiful meal, created by me.

Today's Reminder

If my eyes and heart are opened to receive new impressions, each day will be a new adventure. Even in the monotony of my life, no two days are ever the same and the differences will reveal to me a succession of fresh delights—if I am willing.

> "I ask God to make me willing to
> see clearly my everyday
> experiences, to sharpen my
> perception of how much there is
> to enjoy, even in ordinary things
> and happenings. Let me be
> receptive. Restore to me my
> capacity for wonder."

When will I realize that I need not permit the alcoholic's behavior to confuse my life and destroy my peace of mind? When will I learn that there is no compulsion, in law or ethics, that forces me to accept humiliation, uncertainty and despair. Have I perhaps accepted it because I have a subconscious desire for martyrdom? Do I secretly relish feeling sorry for myself and want sympathy from others?

Today's Reminder

I have a right to free myself from any situation that interferes with my having a decent life and pleasant experiences. Every human being is entitled to live without fear, uncertainty, discomfort. I should take a firm stand and hold fast to whatever decision I make, to help not only myself and my family, but the suffering alcoholic as well. Constant wavering can only hinder me from breaking out of my present thinking patterns.

> "God guide me to make the right decision and give me the fortitude to cling to it against all pressures and persuasions."

If someone dislikes me, or resents something I have done, I ought first to consider whether it was I who generated the dislike or resentment. Was it something I did? Is it something I should make amends for? If so, am I inclined to justify what I did when it really wasn't right? Answering these questions will give me good practice in being honest with myself.

If I was hurtful, and I make excuses to myself for what I did, I am building a *second* wall between me and the person I injured. Let me tear the first wall down by being honest, and honestly acknowledging my fault.

Today's Reminder

What a relief it is to acknowledge that I am only human, that I do make mistakes, and that I am willing to correct them. I can't help liking myself better after the air has been cleared. In solidifying a friendship, I become a better friend to myself.

> "God help me to avoid the temptation to deceive myself by justifying my actions when they were wrong. Make me strong enough to do what I should to keep me serene."

We pray for sobriety for the alcoholic because we believe this will solve all our problems. This is an illusion. Sobriety is only the first step in building a good life. Unless we both work to overcome the emotional conflicts within ourselves, we remain at a standstill. Our troubles only take new forms because they did not stem from alcoholism, but from the personality flaws that caused the alcoholism, and from our irrational reactions to them. Even when the alcoholic has conquered the compulsion to drink, I must remember that I have much to learn about adjusting to the sober alcoholic.

Today's Reminder

I will not delude myself into thinking that sobriety is the sole goal. I will deal with each problem that comes to me with the help of the Twelve Steps and the loving interchange with my friends in Al-Anon.

> "I pray for the wisdom to take a rational and tolerant attitude toward whatever troubles I must face each day."

How can I make myself aware that my weak-kneed acceptance of an unacceptable situation is a reflection on my own self-respect? Am I a milk-sop, a slave, to be pushed around at the will of a sick personality? Is my long-suffering attitude going to achieve any good results? Or will it only reinforce the alcoholic in his belief that he can manipulate the situation to get his own way? Am I being fair to him in allowing him to outmaneuver me at every turn? Will he look for sobriety if I give him no compelling reason to do so—not only for his sake, but for my own?

Today's Reminder

I am an individual with the right to a good life. I must not look to anyone else to make a good life for me; this I must do for myself. Have I deceived myself into thinking that it is my lot to accept anything life chooses to hand out to me, however humiliating or degrading?

> "I pray to learn the way to see myself
> as a child of God, bearing in my heart
> and mind the dignity and grace He has
> conferred upon every one of His children.
> Let me learn to live up to this picture
> of perfection—a little at a time, but
> always going forward."

I learn in Al-Anon that a frank, honest look at my way of handling the alcoholic situation may suddenly show me that I possess, and use, a whole armory of murderous weapons. They are the same weapons used by many spouses: indignation expressed in a strident voice, irresponsible accusations, nagging, tears and hysteria, self-righteousness and many more. These weapons are killers. They kill the alcoholic's desire to find a better way of life. They kill love and respect. They destroy the alcoholic by increasing his already-unbearable guilt. And they destroy us who use such weapons.

Today's Reminder

I will try to clear out of my life and my mind all the tools of destruction I have been using. I know they can do nothing to improve my situation. I will make myself learn to use a new set of tools: tolerance, kindness, patience, courtesy, love and humor—and a firm determination to do what is necessary to improve my life.

> "God, who is all good and
> all wisdom, provides me with the tools
> that are useful in overcoming my
> difficulties. May I be willing to use them,"

I belong to Al-Anon in order to learn how to live at peace with myself and others. To this end I have a responsibility to my group members never to reveal anyone's secrets. I must protect the anonymity of my fellow members and their families. Only in this way can I help my group grow in its capacity to help others. Above all, I will never identify a story by a personal name. Just as I want to be assured that others will not repeat what I say at meetings or what I tell another member in confidence, so I will guard against indiscretion.

Today's Reminder

"Anonymity is the spiritual foundation of all our Traditions, ever reminding us to place principles above personalities." This Twelfth Tradition by which we try to live should be kept in mind by all of us, at all times. It is the secret of success in the Al-Anon way of life.

> "A Talebearer revealeth secrets, but
> he that is of a faithful spirit con-
> cealeth the matter."
>
> (*Proverbs*)

No matter what the problems are that we're trying to cope with, a major source of frustration is trying to encompass too much at once. We forget that we need to deal with only one day at a time, and try to crowd too much into the waking hours of that day—or we even extend it beyond the point of weariness. We can get more out of each hour—and accomplish more—if we try to cope with only as much as is possible in that one day.

We find such relaxed—and relaxing—counsel in the helpful little folder, Just for Today, which gives us, among others, the following:

Today's Reminder

"Just for today I will live through this day only, and not tackle all my problems at once. I can do something for twelve hours that would appall me if I felt I had to keep it up for a lifetime."

I will slow my pace. If I am under pressure and setting myself deadlines and worrying about tomorrow, I will stop for a few minutes and *think* —of just this one day and what I can do with it.

> "For there is a time . . . for every purpose
> and for every work."
>
> (*Ecclesiastes*)

I cannot hurt others without hurting myself. This is a compelling reason for taking thought before I release words that might set off an angry interchange. Have I ever considered that the impulse to say something unkind comes from my own guilt and unease, which erupts in blows against others?

It may be a momentary release for me, but it returns like a boomerang to increase my own discomfort. Impatience with others only generates their impatience with me. Impulsive criticism at an Al-Anon meeting can affect the unity of the group on which I depend for my help.

Today's Reminder

If only I can learn to quiet my mind before I speak! I do not want to act with impatience and hostility, for I know it will react on me. It is a mistake to think this requires self-control; patience can be acquired by learning to *let go of self-will.*

> Jonathan Swift said: "Whoever is out of patience is out of possession of his soul. Men must not turn into bees who kill themselves in stinging others."

If I can see myself clearly and honestly in relation to my present circumstances, I will not become the victim of self-pity or resentment. If I do what I should, I will be at peace with myself.

It is only when I compare my lot in life with that of others that the destructive emotion of self-pity is allowed to engulf me. It is only by taking offense at what others do that I will be afflicted with resentment. If I feel that what I am doing is right, I will not be dependent on the admiration or applause of others. It is gratifying, but not essential to my contentment.

I will learn to judge my own motives, to evaluate my own actions, so that, little by little, I can bring them into line with my standards and ideals.

Today's Reminder

Nothing has the power to hurt my feelings and stir up unwholesome emotions in me unless I allow it. I will do what is given me to do. I will do it as well as I can. That will be my inner security against which all outside battering will be powerless.

> "Labor not as one who is wretched, nor
> yet as one who would be pitied or admired.
> Direct yourself to one thing only, to put
> yourself in motion and to check yourself
> at all times."
>
> (Marcus Aurelius: *Meditations*)

In Al-Anon we are often reminded that what
we pray for may not be what is best for us. We
are able to see only a little way, and our vision
is clouded by our present situation and daily
happenings and distractions.

If the problems I have to face seem beyond
my endurance, I will not explain them to
God; He already knows. I will not tell Him
what I expect Him to do about my difficulties;
He knows what is best for me.

When I am faced with something which it is
beyond my power to perform, to decide, or to
cope with, I will not struggle with it by myself.
I will ask Him to show me what steps to take.
This is prayer: not to ask for anything but
guidance.

Today's Reminder

"All true prayer somehow confesses our absolute
dependence on God. It is a vital contact with Him.
It is when we pray truly that we really are. From
our prayers we receive light to apply . . . to our
own problems and difficulties."

(Thomas Merton: *No Man Is an Island*)

"We, ignorant of ourselves,
  Beg often our own harms,
  Which the Wise Power
  Denies us for our good; so we find profit
  By losing of our prayers."

(Shakespeare: *Antony & Cleopatra*)

Learning the Al-Anon program in all its deep meanings, and applying it to my daily life, is not a simple matter of going to a meeting now and then. Suppose I had decided to learn another language, or study art or a science. I would have to work at it every day and practice the things I learned until they became part of me. A philosopher or an artist studies every day for years to perfect himself. How can I hope to perfect myself in the Al-Anon way of life without daily application?

Today's Reminder

Right now I am reading something that will help me to grasp the Al-Anon philosophy. Right now I will set myself a program of reading the Al-Anon literature, which will help me to understand my problem and improve my outlook on life. Then I will be ready to solve my difficulties as they arise; then I will know when to stand aside and let them work themselves out.

" 'Understanding is a wellspring of life to him that hath it.' (*Proverbs*) I pray for the steadfastness to read, every day, something that will help me to gain understanding."

Did I realize, when I came into Al-Anon, that alcoholism was not something the drinker could control by sheer will-power alone? Of course I didn't! But when I have heard, over and over again, that the alcoholic suffers from a disease, why do I still speak and act toward him as though he were willfully bad? I know, when I reflect on it, that the alcoholic is basically a good and sensitive human being, but until this thought is firmly implanted in my mind, I will be unable to reflect it in my actions.

Today's Reminder

Arguments are useless against a sickness. Compassion and understanding on my part can have the power to heal because they will teach me not to punish. Even if the serenity I acquire in Al-Anon brings no change in the alcoholic, it will at least have strengthened me to face my problems more reasonably.

> "I pray to remember, every day, every hour, and especially in times of crisis, that hostile behavior on my part will only add fuel to a fire that could destroy us both."

Before AA comes into the life of an alcoholic, and before Al-Anon reveals a new way of life to us, correcting one's faults seemed to depend entirely on will-power, directed at *eliminating* them.

Bad habits and compulsions cannot be conquered by determined resolutions or promising ourselves that we won't go on doing this or that. They cannot be *rooted* out—for what would fill that vacuum? They must be *replaced* —with their *opposites*. The secret is to substitute the positive for the negative—the *I will* for the *I won't*.

Today's Reminder

If I am morose and discontented, I will deliberately cultivate happy thoughts. If I am prone to criticize, I will seek out what is good and pleasing and fix my mind on that. I will replace my fruitless doubts and fears with faith and confidence. If I am bored, I will learn something new—even a new way to make the same old chores more enjoyable.

> "I stopped trying to *force*
> myself to eliminate my faults when
> I found it didn't work. Then I realized
> that I had to replace them with something better."

How often we see wives, husbands and parents come to Al-Anon groups because they have reached a point of desperation over the alcoholic drinking of a family member!

When they are told that Al-Anon's purpose is not to bring about sobriety for the alcoholic, but peace of mind and sanity for them, they find it hard to take at first. Gradually the philosophy penetrates and they see the problem more clearly. Yet once the alcoholic is safely in AA and doing well, they often feel they "have it made" and Al-Anon becomes unimportant to them. They do not realize they need Al-Anon as a permanent way of life.

Today's Reminder

Al-Anon is for all those who are living with an alcoholic, whether actively drinking or sober. Unless we realize that, and live that thought, we have missed the whole point and purpose of its beneficent philosophy. To those who get the most out of it, it is truly a way of life.

> "Let me never forget how much Al-Anon can do to make me a better person with a richer, fuller life. It gives me the means and the wisdom to serve others which I must have in order to fulfill myself."

Some of us are still enduring the agonies of living with active alcoholism. We wonder why the alcoholic cannot realize what his drinking is doing to the family. We doubt that he cares. If he did, we think, how could he behave in this irrational way?

In Al-Anon we learn that this is a false conclusion; we cannot know how terribly he suffers from guilt at the hurt he inflicts. His only way of escape from this guilt is to drink again.

Our way to help him is to realize how sick he is and how he himself is hurt by the results of his compulsion. Reproaches and tears only make matters worse. We can have patience and compassion without being a crutch, so he may gain the strength to seek help for himself.

Today's Reminder

If we say to ourselves, "How long, oh Lord, how long?" we are wallowing in self-pity. We have at our command the means of climbing out of the pit we are in if we will but use them.

> ". . . . courage to change the things
> we can."

Living with an alcoholic may bring us to such a point of desperation that we feel God has abandoned us. Our children are disturbed, debts are piling up; encounters with police, imprisonment, infidelity and physical violence may disgrace the family. What can we do? We know it is time for action, but what steps shall we take? Our own thinking is so confused that we are in no condition to make decisions. At such a crisis, we should seek impartial counsel from a source of professional help: a clergyman, a social agency or a Family Court. But most of all it is important to use the Al-Anon suggestion, "Let go and let God."

Today's Reminder

I know I am powerless to deal with my problem by myself. The more I struggle to work it out, the more difficult it becomes. I know that Divine Power can deal with matters which are beyond me. I will try to empty my mind of all fear.

> "God does not deprive us of His love;
> we deprive Him of our cooperation.
> God would never reject me if I had
> not first rejected His love."
>
> (St. Francis de Sales)

Of course I am obligated, by compassion and a common humanity, to help others. But this does not mean I should do for them what they ought to do for themselves. I have no right to deprive anyone else of the challenge to meet his own responsibility. Although mutual dependence is one of the comforts and rewards of marriage, each partner must do his own job, carry his own share of the burden. If the alcoholic member of the family fails in his duties, my assuming them will only weaken his will to accept his share of the responsibility.

Today's Reminder

How can I best help the alcoholic? By not interfering when he gets into difficulties. I must detach myself from his shortcomings, neither making up for them nor criticizing them. Let me learn to play my own role, and leave his to him. If he fails in it, the failure is not mine, no matter what others may think or say about it.

> "For though we are made especially
> for the sake of one another, still
> each of us has his own tasks. Otherwise
> another's faults would harm me,
> which God has not willed, in order
> that my happiness may not depend on
> another."
> (Marcus Aurelius: *Meditations, paraphrased*)

Most of us come to Al-Anon for help as a last resort. We've tried everything else. Perhaps we've seen its effects on others; it seems to have worked like magic, and we want some of that! Then we find out that it isn't magic— it's a kind of spiritual common sense that we must buckle down and learn.

We start, like children in first grade, with the First Step: *Admitted we were powerless over alcohol; that our lives had become unmanageable.* The second part of this Step is easy to admit; but to the first part we usually give only lip service. We find it difficult to surrender to the idea that we, the competent ones who have tried to cope with an alcoholic situation, don't really know how to handle it correctly.

Today's Reminder

Step One must be learned and repeated until it becomes a part of me. Whenever I give in to my natural impulse and habit to take over and try to *force* a change,I'm in trouble again. I know I can only make progress when I really believe in, and practice, the First Step.

"I pray to be released from my compulsion to control my situation. I have so often proved I am unable to control it. Let me think, know and feel my powerlessness; then I will at least learn to let go and let God."

One of the difficulties many of us experience when the alcoholic has turned from The Bottle to AA and sobriety is that we may have just as little companionship as we had before. What good is it, we complain, to have him out every night, whether it's at a bar or an AA meeting?

Al-Anon can be of infinite help to us in correcting this point of view. We learn to see this new way of life in its true light: as an opportunity to relieve ourselves of our feeling of responsibility for the alcoholic, and to recognize and build upon the inner resources on which our personal serenity depends.

Today's Reminder

I prayed for sobriety—and now it's here. Am I using it only to find new reasons for feeling sorry for myself? Wouldn't I be happier if I could now turn my attention to finding ways to enjoy this new life?

> "I pray to understand that the
> adjustment to sobriety is no more
> difficult for me than for the
> alcoholic. Let me look for the
> good things in this new way of life."

"Taking the First Step" is not a matter of reading the words *"admitted* we were power- less . . ." but of impressing them so deeply on our consciousness that the admitting will be established as part of our way of thinking and feeling.

We may read and repeat this Step hundreds of times, and still fail to use it in the way we think and act. If we really *accept* the fact that we have no authority or power over any other human being, we would not try to compel the drinker to do what we want him to.

Have I attained this frame of mind? Can I make myself let go of the problem?

Today's Reminder

I will look back upon all the things I have done to make the alcoholic stop drinking. Has it pro- duced one iota of improvement to scold, weep, complain, accuse, reason, appeal or threaten? Am I any better off today for indulging in these futile gestures? Is the drinker any closer to sobri- ety? Or is the situation worse?

> "I pray for the wisdom to realize
> that progess begins only when
> I am ready to detach myself from the
> idea that I alone can control and solve
> another's problem."

The Second Step of the Twelve is the one that opens the door to understanding and growth. Once we have admitted our helplessness—and our inability to manage our lives—then we are ready to "believe that a Power greater than ourselves could restore us to sanity."

Do I find it shocking to admit that my thinking was not sane, that I reacted in an unreasonable manner to the alcoholic's activities? Let me look back at the First Step for proof! But now I realize there is available to me a Power to which I can turn for help. This is a Power *greater than we are*. If we accept this, we gain a more realistic insight into our relation to the universe.

Today's Reminder

I can attain real dignity, importance and individuality only by admitting my dependence on a Power which is great and good beyond anything I can imagine or understand. I want to use this help in making all my decisions. Even though my little human mind cannot figure out what the outcome will be, I am confident that whatever comes will be for my ultimate good.

> "Thank God I am not dependent on my
> own resources alone. Having tried
> to bring order and meaning into my
> life without God's help, I will
> now step aside and let Him take over."

When I say to myself that I am going to turn all my problems over to God, this does not give me leave to shirk my responsibilities. I have been given certain tools with which to run my life, and the free will to use them. They include judgment, intelligence, good will and the power to reason. Perhaps much of my trouble stems from having misused these tools. Judgment may have been warped by resentment, my intelligence by failure to face issues honestly. Good will can be lost when we are unable to be tolerant of the faults of others. The power to reason can be dulled when we fail to detach ourselves from the emotional content of a problem.

Today's Reminder

When I am desperate enough to ask for help, I will not expect it to come in the form of easy solutions. I must play a part in solving my problems, but my Higher Power will provide the guidance and the strength to take the right action.

> "I pray for the wisdom to understand
> my difficulties clearly and honestly.
> And for the strength to do something
> constructive about them. I know
> I can count on God's help in this."

How often we think that the trials we have to face were caused by outside forces, by fate, or by God. We're only too ready to look outside ourselves for the reasons for our afflictions, when the real enemy is self-deception. We may be poor, deprived of the necessities of life, frustrated in the things we think we want to do. It is only too easy to blame all these things on the alcoholic. Yet however difficult he may make our lives, we could do a great deal to offset this damage by turning our examination and criticism on ourselves, and taking energetic steps to correct what we think and do.

Today's Reminder

I will examine my own attitudes and activities and face the fact that much of what I do—or leave undone—contributes to my distress. Like the alcoholic, I, too, have an unrecognized sense of guilt which I could overcome by correcting what I find wrong with me. My first job is to stop fooling myself, stop excusing my own shortcomings.

> "If we say that we have no fault,
>   we deceive ourselves and the truth
>   is not in us."
>   (*1st Epistle General of John*)

As I uncover and face my own shortcomings, my many good qualities will be revealed to me, too, reminding me that they have the same reality as my faults. Let me appreciate them, for they not only *offset* the faults, but give me a foundation on which to grow. If I recognize that I am kind, tolerant, generous, honest, patient—let me delight in these constructive qualities. They make it possible to accept myself as a friend; they are mighty allies in eliminating the shortcomings that are roadblocks to my serenity.

Today's Reminder

It is just as self-deceptive to discount what is good in us as to justify what is not. This is false humility, which is as hampering as arrogance! The purpose of examining our characters—with as much honesty and detachment as possible—is not to exaggerate guilt for what we lack, but to use the good to overcome the faults.

> "Let me learn to understand myself
> first; that will occupy me so fully
> that I will have no time nor thought
> to analyze and criticize the compulsive
> drinker."

Even after the alcoholic has become sober, I will not expect life to be free from difficulty and worry. I will accept the usual upsets that occur in family life, realizing that they may have come into sharper focus now that they are no longer obscured by The Bottle.

I will take disappointments as they come, always reminding myself that the blessing of sobriety should make them easier to take, if I use them as enriching experiences. This attitude on my part will help to draw our family closer together.

Today's Reminder

Troubles are opportunities to grow, to make us better, not bitter. Rightly used, we can learn from them not to repeat our own mistakes. Once freed from the problem of active alcoholism, we are free to devote ourselves to solving all other problems as they arise.

> "Let me never forget to be grateful
> for the good things in my life, and
> especially for the sobriety that will
> help restore our whole family to
> sanity and serenity."

Somehow it makes my own burdens easier to live with when I hear the stories of others at Al-Anon meetings. Sharing experience, strength and hope acts like a medicine on the spirit, giving us a perspective on ourselves and our woes. We see how much worse off others are, and are able to help them by listening, and giving them some of the strength we have gained from the Al-Anon program. The coming together of various personalities and points of view, responding to each other in the light of the Al-Anon philosophy, is a very real therapy.

Today's Reminder

When I am "too tired" to go to an Al-Anon meeting, do I realize I am depriving myself of stimulation and refreshment of spirit? I may miss hearing a single chance phrase that would throw new light on my own problem; or I may miss an opportunity to help someone else.

> "I pray that each day may advance my steps on the road to understanding; that I may leave nothing undone that could have changed the course of my life for the better."

When we first come into Al-Anon, we are astonished at the number of cheerful, smiling people we see in the group. We think it isn't possible that they're having such problems as ours—only to discover that many of them are much worse off than we are.

After a time, after a succession of meetings, we begin to discover what has given them such an optimistic outlook, for we begin to share in the secret—and use it in our own daily lives.

Today's Reminder

What the Al-Anon program has done for others, it can do for me—if I listen and absorb what I hear and use it every day. I do not go merely for the relief of airing my own problems, but to learn from others how to deal with them.

> "I pray to be led into a new way of
> thinking about the difficulties I
> have to face. A new point of view
> will put them into perspective and
> reduce them to manageable size. I
> pray especially to resist exaggerat-
> ing my troubles until they overwhelm
> me."

Would it help my situation to know why the alcoholic drinks to such excess that everything around him is damaged in some way by his compulsion? If he drinks to drown out the pain of shattering childhood experiences, which he does not even identify or remember, how can such pain be located and removed? Certainly not by us; we are amateurs—and emotionally-involved amateurs at that! It would take years and thousands of dollars worth of psychiatry—and even then the outcome would be uncertain. But at least the knowledge that he suffers should keep me from condemning him.

Today's Reminder

It is enough for me to know that the unhappy drinker can get help in AA, where so many have found contented sobriety. It is enough for me to know I can overcome my own confusion by using the Al-Anon program.

> "Let me conduct myself and my life
> in such a way that I will have no
> reason to reproach myself for making
> a bad situation worse. This, at
> least, is within my power: *to make
> it better*."

I went into Al-Anon, as so many of us do, with an overwhelming desire to pour out my troubles, to talk, talk, talk. It was like a dammed-up river that suddenly burst its banks. And, although it gave me some relief, it left behind an emptiness, a certain dissatisfaction.

Then one day I realized why this was. When I talk all the time, nothing new is being added to me. I am using the same old destructive thought material that has kept me at a standstill for so long.

To absorb new ideas, I keep my lips closed and my ears open. I find this gives me a new perspective on my problems, so solutions come more easily.

Today's Reminder

Al-Anon meetings are a wellspring of helpful thoughts; if I don't listen, I don't receive them. Constant talking would deprive me of the help I am seeking in Al-Anon. Should I stand in my own light in this way?

> "I pray to be reminded that Al-Anon
> has important gifts for me that I
> can receive only by holding my peace
> and letting others talk."

The First Step is a clear and ringing statement of our true status in the alcoholic situation. It should leave no doubt in our minds as to just where *we* stand. Reading the first half, *admitting we are powerless over alcohol,* might generate instant resistance in our minds. The automatic response may be: "Not me, *I'm* not powerless. I'll fix this." But the Step goes on to say: "our lives have become unmanageable." This challenge *denies* that we are able to do any fixing. For haven't we, ourselves, demonstrated beyond doubt that we have not been competent to manage our lives?

Today's Reminder

The First Step is by no means a statement of despair. It merely points out our human limitations. It prepares us to become humble, so we can find the spiritual answers that will place our lives on an entirely different plane. It is preparing us for deliverance from problems we cannot cope with alone.

> "Let not my stubborn self-will stand
> in the way of my achieving serenity
> Before I can accomplish anything,
> I must accept my need for help."

What happens when the constructive ideas I am exposed to in Al-Anon just roll off my consciousness? Why don't they penetrate my mind? Why can't I absorb them, so they'll really work for me?

One of our slogans is a single word: THINK. How can I do that if all I do is *talk*? I can benefit from the Steps and the Slogans only if I *think* about them. I can learn from others only if I learn to keep silent, and *think* about what I am hearing. The compulsive talkers among us are those who get the least help from the Al-Anon program, and make the least progress.

Today's Reminder

I will construct my share of the conversation thoughtfully, remembering that its purpose is to help someone else, as well as to help me think more clearly. I will listen to others and extract helpful, enlightening ideas from what they say.

> "I pray to acquire the habit of
> listening, confining my own talk
> to what might be of help to others.
> Teach me the use of silence."

In Al-Anon we start by clearing out the debris of our own mistakes. We learn to recognize how much we ourselves have contributed to the destruction of our home life.

This was no vacuum we were living in, with only the alcoholic doing all the damage. *We* reacted, too, and made things worse. We are asked, here in Al-Anon, to reflect on our own conduct. Did we talk too much, too loudly and hysterically, when we should have kept silence? Did we oppress the unhappy drinker still further at hangover time, with a black and sulking silence, when a few comforting words might have turned his thoughts toward looking for help?

Today's Reminder

How difficult it is to face our own shortcomings! How much easier it becomes when we face them together in Al-Anon, since many of us have been guilty, unknowingly, of the same mistakes.

> "Make me grateful for having been
> shown a way out of my difficulties
> through the Al-Anon program of
> *self*-understanding. Make me humble
> enough to accept a new and more
> rational view of my life."

In Al-Anon we have a familiar expression: "to *work* the program." It means what it says; it benefits us to exactly the degree that we *work* at it.

What does *working the program* mean? It means to attend meetings faithfully; to read some Al-Anon literature every day, and to apply what we learn to our everyday living. And very important, it means sharing with others what we are learning and using, and accepting with an open mind what they share with us.

We do not come to Al-Anon meetings to be amused, entertained or shocked with horror stories, but to discuss Al-Anon ideas—to think deeply and reflectively about what we hear and to talk constructively and clearly in order to help others.

Today's Reminder

I have placed my confidence in Al-Anon. I will not look to others to do my work for me while I'm "too busy" or "too tired" to do my reading and attend meetings and keep in touch with my fellow members. Al-Anon can do much for me, but I must help, too.

> "I pray to be freed from *indifference*.
> I need a strong conviction that Al-Anon,
> too, has the most to give to those who
> really want to help themselves."

One of the most inspiring and encouraging things that happens at Al-Anon meetings is an expression of heartfelt gratitude from a member. For those who are hopeless and despairing, such a message as this gives a foretaste of lightened burdens:

"Life begins to make a great deal of sense to me since I came to Al-Anon. The world is beginning to reveal its beauty which for a long time was obscured by my worrying over my troubles. I am learning to deal with them now, and what makes it easier is that I deal only with the problems that are mine. I am learning I cannot carry another's burdens, no matter how much I love him."

Today's Reminder

One of Al-Anon's important fringe benefits is that it increases my awareness of the world around me, so I can see and enjoy it. This alone helps to dim the difficulties I had been concentrating on, creating my own misery.

"After a time in Al-Anon, we discover we are acquiring a sense of reality which is absolutely essential to serenity."

Alcoholism is a disease—we hear this statement over and over again. This is so hard for most of us to accept because we cannot associate it with germs or viruses, as in other "respectable" diseases. Nevertheless, we will see substantial progress in ourselves once we realize that it is a physical, mental and spiritual illness that has no single isolated cause. I cannot stop it, any more than I can make a sick person get well.

Compulsive drinking is an outward manifestation of the alcoholic's inner anguish; if it goes on, it becomes a destructive cycle of deterioration. To make myself ready to help, I must, first of all, accept alcoholism as an illness.

Today's Reminder

How does the knowledge that the alcoholic is sick work on me? It changes my attitude toward him! It replaces my rage and frustration with quiet patience. It lets me choose *the right moment* to suggest AA—when he is truly in despair and willing to acknowledge his need for help.

"I pray for the realization that
  the alcoholic is sick and desperate,
  and I ask that I be given the strengtn to help him
  in the right and constructive way."

When violent quarrels take place in the home, both partners fail to realize that their intense involvement with each other can destroy what should be a sacred relationship. With those who are closest to us, we are most apt to forget the consideration we owe to one another. We learn, in Al-Anon, that we can set a new tone in the home by such a simple thing as courtesy—consistent, gentle courtesy, to every member of the family, including the littlest one.

Today's Reminder

A quiet, composed response to an enraged attack can "take the wind out of the sails" of the attacker like so much magic. What can I possibly lose by trying it? At least it will add to my own dignity and stature to say nothing I will later regret.

> "Of Courtesy: it is much less
>   Than courage of heart or holiness.
>   Yet in my walks it seems to me
>   That the grace of God is in Courtesy."
>   (Hilaire Belloc: *Courtesy*)

The Al-Anon program will work for anyone who approaches it with an open mind. We cannot expect miracles overnight; it took years to create the situation in which we find ourselves today.

I will keep myself receptive and listen. I will not be quick to judge and say: "Yes, but my case is so different." The details may differ, but basically my story is the same as that of all those who live with the problem of alcoholism.

I must cling to this one thought: Al-Anon can change my life—if I give it a chance.

Today's Reminder

If I take to myself each day even one small new idea, heard at a meeting or read in Al-Anon literature, I will make progress. Things may not work out as I *want* them to, but as my point of view changes, what I *thought* I wanted changes, too. My ultimate contentment does not depend on having things work out my way.

> "We may think we can change the things
> around us according to our desires, but
> when a solution does come, we find it
> was our desires that had changed."

Once upon a time a Frightened Woman came to Al-Anon with a shocking story. Her husband was violent and often beat her, there was never enough money for food, he tangled with the police, and time after time they were evicted for not paying their rent.

She might never have had the courage to come to Al-Anon if her husband hadn't been away in jail.

After she began to acquire a bit of confidence, she wondered whether it might not be better after all to take radical action. One day she asked her sponsor, "Shall I get a divorce?"

Her sponsor said: "This is a decision only you can make. Other wives might have given up long ago. But are you ready for a complete break? What does your heart tell you?"

Without hesitation, the woman said: "By all right and reason I know I should separate myself permanently from him, but you see, I love him."

She had found her own answer, as all of us must. Who can understand it? Who is wise enough to make a decision for another? Surely none of us in Al-Anon, for we are taught that no situation is really hopeless.

As it turned out, this one was not, either. As she overcame her fear of her husband, self-pity yielded, too. She stopped involving herself in his disasters, and taking part in arguments that used to end in violence. Her husband was compelled to face his own problems, and happily, he learned to face them in AA.

I live with an alcoholic. Whether still drinking or not, the situation calls for patience, acceptance and resolution. How do I acquire and practice these qualities? By detaching myself emotionally from the problems I encounter each day. Or, to put it another way, by not allowing myself to become involved emotionally.

This is not easy. I will try to be more objective and not take personally everything that is said or done. I will read every piece of literature I can find on Al-Anon, so I will be better informed to re-educate my own thinking habits.

Today's Reminder

Each day I will review my progress in emotional detachment. What did I say that would have been better unsaid? Did my detachment take form in a discreet, friendly silence, or in reproachful sulking? Did I miss an opportunity to say a helping word at the right moment?

> "I pray for the enlightenment
> to make my detachment loving,
> not cruel. Let it not be a
> wall between us, but a bond
> of mutual respect for one
> another's individuality."

We punish ourselves far more than life ever punishes us. It takes some time before we realize that we have considerable power to change our lives, if we are willing to use it.

I will start by rooting out the doubts and fears that grew so great when my spouse was drinking alcoholically. Even after long sobriety, do I not occasionally wonder whether it will last? Does unexpected lateness make me suspicious that "something's going on?" Why do I punish myself in this way? Why don't I accept God's gift of mental sobriety which is mine for the taking, along with contentment and serenity?

Today's Reminder

Mental sobriety is a state of reasonableness, rational judgment, balance. It is emotional sickness when we continue to be apprehensive and anxious when we really have no reason to doubt.

> "I will pray today and every day,
> for healthful, wholesome thinking,
> so that I may not generate
> trouble for myself."

Do I occasionally remind myself that the newcomer to Al-Anon is desperate, lonely and bewildered? When I see a new face at a meeting, and it is my turn to make a comment, do I keep that newcomer in mind, and say something to inspire hope?

Those who are familiar with the Al-Anon "language" and the Al-Anon concepts are apt to forget that they may increase the newcomer's bewilderment instead of encouraging him or her to come back to us for help.

Let me cultivate *awareness* of those around me; it is all the better for me, too, if I clarify my thoughts before I speak.

Today's Reminder

I want to keep in mind that the Al-Anon therapy is an *interchange*. The more help I give, the more I get. If I learn to be aware of others, and am conscious of their reactions, the practice I get in this way will help me improve my relationships at home, too.

> "The mouth of the just bringeth
> forth wisdom; the lips of the
> righteous know what is acceptable."
> (*Proverbs*)

"Detach!" we are told in Al-Anon. This does not mean detaching ourselves, and our love and compassion, from the alcoholic. Detachment, in the Al-Anon sense, means to realize we are individuals. We are not bound morally to shoulder the alcoholic's responsibilities.

Detachment from the problems caused by compulsive drinking shows us the futility of covering up for the alcoholic, keeping up a brave front, being ashamed or apologetic for situations not of our making. Once we can hold back from such complete involvement, we will have a new sense of freedom and strength.

Today's Reminder

I will not permit myself to become emotionally involved in matters that should not be my concern. I will not interfere with the working out of another's difficulties, however dear and close we may be to each other. Detachment is essential to any healthy relationship between people. Each of us is a free individual, with neither one in control of the other.

> "For what knowest thou, O wife,
> whether thou shalt save thy husband?
> Or how knowest thou, O man, whether
> thou shalt save thy wife? As the
> Lord hath called every one, so let
> him walk."
>
> *(1st Corinthians)*

Have I ever sought to find the tiny spark that detonated a family row that brought into the open ugly words and violent recriminations? Can I admit that I may have caused it by being too quick to react to a ridiculous accusation or denunciation? Do I take everything the alcoholic says—in his frustrated rage against *himself*—as an offense to me?

When the guilt of the alcoholic explodes, I must realize that it is always aimed at those nearest, and often dearest. I want to remind myself that such outbursts only reveal the drinker's own unhappiness. I will not make the situation worse by taking seriously what the alcoholic says at such times.

Today's Reminder

A long-ago childhood chant provides a simple answer: "Sticks and stones can break my bones, but names can never hurt me." Unless *we* let them.

Let me learn to keep peace with silence
when it is not the right time to say what comes
to mind."

" '. . . There is a time to keep
silence and a time to speak'

(*Ecclesiastes*)

I will accept the fact that sobriety does not bring a complete transformation. After all, the alcoholic is still basically the same person, with the same individuality. The one immediate difference, of course, is that his personality is not distorted by drunkenness. But if sometimes he is moody and uncommunicative, I will understand that he is having a hard time adjusting to his new way of life. I will not let myself forget how, in the past, such uneasiness could drive him back to the bottle. I will be grateful for the sobriety. It is the first essential step in restoring us both to a contented, normal state.

Today's Reminder

When other things now trouble me in our relationship, I will remember how ardently I wished and prayed that the alcoholic might be released from the compulsion to drink. Now that sobriety has been realized, I will be patient with all that disturbs me. No matter what other difficulties interpose themselves between me and my serenity, I will hold on to my faith in ultimate good.

> ". . . the trying of your faith worketh
> patience. But let patience have her
> perfect work, that you may be perfect
> and entire, wanting nothing."
>   (*The Epistle General of James*)

When a fellow member in Al-Anon is the victim of cruelty, violence and deprivation, our aroused sympathies often tempt us to give advice. We may see so clearly that the situation is beyond human dignity, yet we must realize that not everyone has the strength of purpose to take decisive action or to make radical changes in their way of life.

If I urge someone to do *what I think I would do* in a similar crisis, and my advice is acted upon, the outcome may be an even greater tragedy, and I would be responsible for that.

The help I *can* give is to offer the thought that no one *needs* to feel trapped—that we do have choices in every situation.

Today's Reminder

I do not know what course of action is right for anyone else. I can offer only comfort and compassion, and the good example of the life I am trying to build.

> "Finally, be ye all of one mind,
>   having compassion one of another,
>   not rendering evil for evil.
> For he that will love
>   life and see good days, let him
>   refrain his tongue from evil and
>   his lips that they speak no guile."
>   (*1st Peter*)

Eventually, if I listen attentively enough at meetings, and read my Al-Anon literature with real concentration, I will absorb the new point of view I need. When I ask: "Why does he drink when he knows it damages him and his family?" I really mean: "How can he *justify* what he is doing?", implying a condemnation I have no right to make. Al-Anon teaches me that the drinker knows no more about his compulsion than I do. I know he suffers from it, too. I will not waste time and energy trying to "figure out the alcoholic." I will concentrate on figuring out why I do what *I* do.

Today's Reminder

Trying to analyze why another person persists in destructive behavior cannot help me out of my own difficulties. I can overcome them only by turning my thoughts inward, to face my own mistakes and to learn how to improve myself. The alcoholic is not my problem. My problem is *me*.

"Although all men have a common destiny, each individual also has to work out his personal salvation for himself. . . . We can help one another find out the meaning of life. . . . But in the last analysis, each is responsible for 'finding himself'."

(Thomas Merton: *No Man Is an Island*)

We are advised to detach our minds and emotions from the problems created by alcoholism. This does not mean detachment from the alcoholic, who needs our loving understanding. When I learn to disentangle myself from a difficulty, it will be easier to think it through. I will remind myself to pause and analyze. This will keep me from impulsive decisions and give me time to devise *constructive* action. Each time this happens, it may seem a small conquest, but each helps me to build a serene stability.

Today's Reminder

I look forward to the time when I can say with confidence: "In Al-Anon I became able to cope with the realities of my life."

A true sense of reality comes only when we can put all the elements of our lives into the correct perspective.

> "God, guide my thoughts and let
> these guide my actions."

It is not surprising that many of us regard as miracles the marvelous changes we see in our Al-Anon friends. It is living proof that Al-Anon does work. It transforms desperate, unhappy people into joyous, useful ones, often long before there has been any decisive change in the alcoholic situation.

Al-Anon produces a change of attitude in us; it gives us perspective on our problems and shrinks them down to manageable size. As we learn to depend upon our Higher Power through applying the Al-Anon program to our lives, fear and uncertainty are replaced by faith and confidence. That is the miracle which we can bring about.

Today's Reminder

This day and every day, I will place myself and my life in the hands of God, secure in the knowledge that He will not fail me, if I, too, do my part.

> "He hath delivered my soul in peace
>   from the battle that was against me:
> for there were many with me."
>
> *(Psalms)*

We are told in Al-Anon that there can be no progress without humility. This idea is confusing to many at first, and it almost always encounters a stubborn resistance in us. "What!" we say, "am I supposed to be a submissive slave to my situation, and accept everything that comes, however humiliating?" No. True humility does not mean meek surrender to an ugly, destructive way of life. It means surrender to God's will, which is quite a different thing. Humility prepares us for the realization of God's will for us; it shows us the benefits we gain from doing away with self-will. We finally understand how this self-will has actually contributed to our distress.

Today's Reminder

The attitude of true humility confers dignity and grace on us, and strengthens us to take intelligent spiritual action in solving our problems.

> "Humble yourselves, therefore, under
> the mighty hand of God. . . . casting all
> your care upon Him, for He careth for
> you. He giveth grace to the humble."
>
> (1st Peter)

Al-Anon meetings are full of surprises. The
people who are smiling and gratefully reviewing their blessings may be the very ones who
have the grimmest problems at home. Yet they
have the courage to turn their minds away
from them and come to Al-Anon to learn and
to help others. How have they found this
serenity? It must be because they do not depend on their own limited resources, but on a
Power greater than themselves in Whom they
have confidence. I will work toward acquiring
this gift of serenity, and see to it that my
actions also speak for my inward faith.

Today's Reminder

It is the difference in *people,* and not in the
severity of their trials, that shows most dramati-
cally in Al-Anon. This should prove to me that the
way we *approach* our problems is important, however they may have overwhelmed us before we
learned how to deal with them.

"With Divine help I will accept what I
cannot change—with courage, composure,
and good humor."

During the dreadful drinking days, the anxiety over what was happening in our family was certainly the most important thing in the world to us. How could it be otherwise? We were living with it, saddled with it. We knew there was a world outside, where people lived in some degree of order and peace, but if we thought about it at all, it was with only a passing pang of envy. We were swamped, drowned, in troubles that left no room for thinking of anything else.

In Al-Anon we discover there is a way out of the most hopeless-seeming situation. We find friends to give us help and encouragement; we find opportunity to help others. And so, slowly, we climb out of the pit in which we thought we were buried.

Today's Reminder

When it suddenly dawns on us that Al-Anon has something we can use, we leap from hopelessness to hope and confidence. We give up despair, we catch a glimpse of hope—and then we *know*. It is up to us to make it work in our lives.

> "Let me realize that the Al-Anon
> program is not a magic potion that
> will instantly cure all my ills,
> but a pattern of living that will
> serve me to exactly the degree
> that I work at it."

I will not be dismayed if life doesn't run smoothly, even when I am confident the active phase of alcoholism is past and we are each developing our lives in the Twelve Step program, I in Al-Anon, my spouse in AA. Although our many upheavals and disagreements may have made a rift between us, we can now look forward to a new life as a contented family unit.

I must still guard against impatience, lapses into feeling sorry for myself, resenting the words and actions of others. Above all, I must not permit myself the tormenting excursions into the bitter past. But now that I am alert to the danger signals, I know I am improving day by day.

Today's Reminder

I will start each day with prayers of gratitude that so much has been accomplished. I know that my Higher Power will continue to provide His light of wisdom in my striving for serenity.

> "Truly the light is sweet, and
> a pleasant thing it is for the
> eyes to behold the sun."
>
> (*Ecclesiastes*)

It was quite a while before I came to realize that the Twelve Steps and the Serenity Prayer could be applied to all my problems, whether or not they were related to alcoholism. Now that I try to use these helps every day, my life seems to move from one miracle to another! I know the joy of beginning each day expectantly, confident that it will hold good things for me. And if a crisis arises, or any problem baffles me, I hold it up to the light of the Serenity Prayer and extract its sting before it can hurt me.

Today's Reminder

When we are strengthened by the Al-Anon philosophy, we find ourselves able to look at things in their proper perspective. We don't let them get too close to us, lest they take on fearsome proportions that do not reflect their real character.

> "I pray to accept, with a serene mind,
> the things I cannot change, knowing it
> is futile to be obstinate about the
> inevitable. I pray to be
> resolute to take action in
> things that must be changed."

Once upon a time three wives of alcoholics decided to meet to learn about Al-Anon. Soon others in the same dilemma came to join them and they became a flourishing group. A number of members who were really putting the program to work had the joy of seeing their husbands join AA.

Then one member stayed away from meetings, and then another, and another. When somebody called them to find out why, they said they were disappointed in Al-Anon because of the way personal, confidential matters had been gossiped about, causing difficulties in the families.

When the culprit was found and reproached, she said in great surprise: "But I only told my husband!"

What we hear in an Al-Anon meeting, and privately from our Al-Anon friends, is meant only to help *us*. It must be kept locked in our hearts, just as we want to be sure others are keeping locked up what we tell them.

Outside our fellowship, I will allow myself to speak only of Al-Anon principles, never of personalities. My success with the program depends on each person's discretion.

> "Anonymity is the spiritual
> foundation of all our
> Traditions, ever reminding
> us to place principles
> above personalities."
>
> (*Tradition Twelve*)

Many long-time Al-Anon members have observed that the newcomer who has what a famous theologian calls "the gift of faith" is apt to grasp the Al-Anon program much more readily than those who try, with grim determination, to "make it on their own."

Faith in a Power greater than we are helps us to use the Al-Anon idea with more confidence and result. For those of us who have lost our faith, or who have always had to struggle along without it, it is often helpful just to accept, blindly and with no reservations. We need not believe, at first; we need not be convinced. If we can only accept, we find ourselves becoming gradually aware of a force for good that is always there to help us.

Today's Reminder

The very act of surrender to a God who is wiser and more powerful than we are can help to bring order into our lives. It serves as a steadying influence and constant guide to right decisions.

> "For what if some did not believe?
> Shall their unbelief make the faith
> of God without effect?"
>
> (*Romans*)

When my heart and mind were filled with discouragement, there was no room for concern for others. Daily I tormented myself, thinking in circles, deciding first on one desperate measure, then another. There was no air, no breathing space, between me and my problem; we were entangled and confused. I could see nothing straight and clear, nothing was revealed in its true colors, only the flaming red of constant hysteria and apprehension. To have found a way out of this kind of thinking is a miracle in itself; I found that miracle in Al-Anon. My own problems were brought into focus by relating them to those of others. I found I could give some thought and compassion to them, and then I began to have peace of mind.

Today's Reminder

It is the sharing of experience and hope that makes our Al-Anon contacts so important to us. Every time we read something about how Al-Anon works, every time we attend a meeting or talk with a fellow member by telephone, we grow in serenity and strength.

> "Let me accept all the rich comfort
> available to me in this way of life,
> for I know it can help me in all
> life's trials."

Losing my temper—call it an "attack of anger"—can be a disease, too. It afflicts many of us before (and even after) we come into Al-Anon. We try to cure this disease by applying the Al-Anon program to our thinking. The symptom of the anger-sickness is an uncontrollable impulse to judge and condemn someone else. In this emotional explosion I am really asserting that everything *I* think and do is right, and everything the other person does is wrong. If I were not sick when I denounce and accuse, I would at least realize that the momentary relief I get from my outburst is poor pay for the consequences I must bear.

Today's Reminder

I learn in Al-Anon to be good to myself. Am I not ill when I allow anger to destroy my poise and peace of mind? When I lose control, am I not handing over control to the one I am treating like an adversary? Can anger ever express love?

> "I pray for quietness to help me
> cure my own emotional instability.
> Let me use serenity to cushion the
> impact of whatever happens outside
> of me."

Why did I come into Al-Anon? Most of us came because we were desperate, lonely, bewildered about the alcoholic's behavior.

The important thing to consider is this: Am I desperate enough to try the Twelve Steps, even if I don't believe anything is wrong with *me*? I came wanting to find out how to change my spouse, and the first thing I was told was that the only person I can possibly change is myself. If I really want a new way of life, I will first look deep within myself and admit my own shortcomings.

Today's Reminder

It is not the alcoholic who is my responsibility. My job is to do something about my own faults, my own part in the mess our life has become. Can I admit that my own irrational behavior helped to create the mess? I am sure I will realize it in time, with the help of Al-Anon.

> "I pray for humility to accept
> the fact that I need help, and
> for the firmness of purpose to
> take action to get it. I ask
> for the aid of my Higher Power
> in striving for a better way of
> life."

During the days of the active alcoholism, every problem loomed so large that I was overwhelmed by it. It was the most important thing in the world. It was the final calamity. Hysteria was in charge. I must have known there was a world outside all this—a sane, comfortable way of living. But this was way beyond me while I was wrestling with my daily shocks and despairs. Now that I have found Al-Anon, I look at my problems with a better sense of proportion and balance. I see problems worse than mine which my friends in Al-Anon handle with poise and courage. Thus my difficulties are scaled down to normal size; I know I can do something about them.

Today's Reminder

Now that I am in Al-Anon, I am no longer alone. I have learned to comfort and encourage others, and that gives me a fresh approach to my own difficulties. I can help others, and they can help me.

> "Woe to him that is alone when he falleth, for he hath not another to help him up."
> (*The Wisdom of Solomon—Apocrypha*)

The longer I am in Al-Anon, the more clearly I perceive that alcoholism is indeed a sickness, a compulsion, an obsession. But haven't I, too, been afflicted with a sick compulsion? Wasn't I determined to "save" the alcoholic, and that to the same degree as he was addicted to alcohol? No wonder the situation became an impasse, with the irresistible force, *me*, trying to move the immovable object, *alcoholism*.

I must remind myself daily that I can save only myself. It is vital to my well-being, and that of my family, to keep myself from going down the road of self-pity, resentment and despair. I now know that I cannot live another person's life.

Today's Reminder

When I devote myself to correcting my own shortcomings and mistakes, it cannot possibly have an adverse effect on the alcoholic. He has the same right and obligation to work out his problems as I have to work out mine. The hands-off policy suggested in Al-Anon is much more likely to strengthen his desire to seek help.

> "I pray that I may learn it is not my function to direct or control another person, however close to me. I will also cease to be a crutch. I can live nobody's life but my own."

Doubts and fears that the sober alcoholic may not keep his sobriety are contrary to the Al-Anon way of thinking. Do we let ourselves doubt that "he'll make the program?" Are we uneasy when he gets home later than expected? Do we jump to the conclusion that he has started drinking again? This we must overcome! Such an attitude cannot be concealed and our lack of confidence can do untold damage. The person who is trying to maintain sobriety needs our loving trust. Even if a relapse *should* happen, the injury is not to us, but to the unfortunate who once again was overcome by the compulsion to drink. This is a time to stand by with patience and compassion. Let us not punish the alcoholic or ourselves.

Today's Reminder

I will carefully guard my own mental sobriety. This gift from my Higher Power will express itself in a quiet, reasonable attitude, regardless of what happens.

> "I pray that I may not fall into the
> error of anticipating trouble. If
> it should come, let me meet it with
> equanimity and love."

Even those of us who have no particular religious faith, or who have lost faith we once had, may reach such extremities that we cry out in desperation for help. We pray involuntarily, we pray to Something, some unknown power, to relieve us of our unbearable burdens.

Before I found Al-Anon, in my confusion and despair I asked for help in this way, but the next moment I would begin to worry again about what was going to happen next. If we do finally ask for God's help, we must do so with absolute confidence. It is fruitless to take back into our own hands the problem which our powerlessness forced us to turn over to Him.

Today's Reminder

We are imprisoned by our own inability or unwillingness to reach out for help to a Power greater than ourselves. I will set myself free from the prison of self-will and pride which I myself have built. I will accept freedom.

> "With the help of my God, I
> shall leap over the wall."
> *(Book of Common Prayer)*

When I started in Al-Anon, I thought of the meetings only as a place where I could unburden myself of my troubles. But I soon learned that complaining about our oppressions and indignities only makes them loom larger and more disturbing. This became clear to me when I heard other members monopolize the time and attention of the group with indignant, woeful recitals of the alcoholic's misbehavior. I see this was not "working the Al-Anon program." I am learning to put the shortcomings of others out of my mind and think constructively about putting Al-Anon ideas to work in my life.

Today's Reminder

I go to Al-Anon to get rid of self-pity and resentment, not to increase their power to destroy me. I go to learn how others have dealt with their problems, so I can apply this wisdom to my own life.

> "I ask God to keep me from
> magnifying my troubles by
> harping on them continually."

Acceptance and surrender are the two attitudes that open all doors to us in the Al-Anon way of living. Yet they are the most difficult for many of us to acquire. No matter how badly we think life has beaten us, we still cling to the idea that acceptance and surrender are a kind of hopeless giving-in, a weakness of character. Not so! *Acceptance* means simply admitting there are things we cannot change. Accepting them puts an end to our futile struggles and frees our thought and energy to work on things that can be changed. Surrender means relinquishing our self-will and accepting God's will and His help.

Today's Reminder

I do not have to accept the continous misery that goes with alcoholism. I will not surrender to the vagaries and machinations of the alcoholic. No one can distort my thinking unless I permit it.

> "God help me to accept the
> responsibility for finding
> a better way of life through
> surrendering to You and Your
> guidance."

There was once an Al-Anon group that never had more than nine members, although there were four AA groups within a couple of miles!

All but three of the nine—the three who had started the group—changed very often. When they dropped out, the old-timers would shrug and say: "What can you do? They just don't realize how Al-Anon could help them."

At meetings there were usually plenty of horror stories about what the alcoholics said and did, and detailed descriptions of sufferings. It was all quite exciting, but nothing much happened to make the newcomers aware of the Al-Anon program and how they could apply it. Nobody kept in touch between meetings, excepting, of course, the three old-timers.

Al-Anon is a program of *self*-improvement. It is nourished by the friendship and concern of all the members for each other and from discussion, *in depth*, of Al-Anon principles in the Twelve Steps, the Twelve Traditions and the slogans.

> "If my life is in chaos, I will look into myself for the cause and cure and use the Twelve Steps to improve my shortcomings. If our group is not a living, functioning unit, we will look for the cause and cure in our Twelve Traditions."

Living with an alcoholic distorted my thinking in many ways, but particularly in one: I
blamed all my problems on The Bottle. Now I
am learning in Al-Anon to look squarely at
each difficulty, not seeking whom to "blame"
but to discover how my attitude helped to
create my problem, or aggravate it.

I must learn to face the consequences of my
own actions and words, and to correct myself
when I am wrong. Accepting responsibility is
essential to becoming mature. Whether the
alcoholic is drinking or not, I will not look for
a scapegoat to excuse my own faults.

Today's Reminder

There is no advantage, no profit, no growth, in
deceiving myself merely to escape the consequences of my own mistakes. When I realize this,
I know I will be making progress.

> "We must be true inside, true to ourselves,
> before we can know a truth that is outside
> us. But we make ourselves true inside by
> manifesting the truth as we see it."
> (Thomas Merton: *No Man Is an Island*)

Who knows whether tomorrow will be good or not. Yet we who live with alcoholics are so prone to expect the worst!

Al-Anon is a twenty-four hour program. This gives us the comforting assurance that we need not burden ourselves with the woes of the past, nor anticipate those that may come in the future.

I will keep always in mind that *today* is my sole concern, and that I will make it as good a day as I can. This one small span of time is mine, and I will use it to do the things that need doing, and have a little time over for enjoyment and reflection.

Today's Reminder

Living one day at a time, and consciously dividing my time into useful and satisfying activities, can give me the variety that is said to be the spice of life. This has the added benefit of keeping my mind off my problems, which often proves the easiest and most logical way to solve them!

> "I will make this day a happy one,
> for I alone can determine what
> kind of a day it will be."

The Higher Power we read about in the
Twelve Steps is a *Spiritual idea.* We may think
of this Higher Power as God—Goodness,
Power, Love, Spirit, Father, Friend. Or it may
be nothing more than the Al-Anon group
where we are at last finding ourselves. Because
we are willing to acknowledge that something
or someone is greater than we are, it becomes
a spiritual idea. The very fact of our surrender,
our humility, makes it spiritual. Things really
begin to happen in our lives when we accept
the idea that there is a power bigger and wiser
than we are. Something begins to happen
when we turn to a spiritual idea for our daily
guidance.

Today's Reminder

It is my confidence in a Higher Power, working
in me, which releases and activates my ability to
make my life a more joyous, satisfying experience.
I cannot bring this about by relying on myself
and my own limited ideas.

> "Let every soul be subject unto
> the higher powers, for there is
> no power but of God."

> (*Romans*)

People whose problems have brought them to the point of despair often try Al-Anon as a last resort. Filled with thoughts of their unhappiness, their whole idea is to talk it all out. Fortunate is the newcomer who finds a group that permits the relief of such expression. It gives others something by which to measure their own progress. It gives them a chance to express compassion, to give encouragement and hope. But still more fortunate is the newcomer to a group that does not allow such unburdening to continue, meeting after meeting. There is work to be done, new ideas to be learned, and for that the problems of yesterday and the fears for tomorrow must be put out of the way.

Today's Reminder

Al-Anon is not a sounding board for continually reviewing our miseries, but a way to learn to detach ourselves from them. I will learn by listening, by reading Al-Anon literature and by trying to live the Twelve Steps.

> "The more I immerse myself in
> Al-Anon teachings, the more I
> will get from them and the more
> I can help others."

Worrying is a usual condition with those of us who are new in Al-Anon. Worry has become such a habit that we can't shake it off, even when our *minds* are convinced that it serves no purpose. We think about what happened yesterday and we're sure it's a clue to the awful things that are sure to happen tomorrow. The members of AA have set us a good example in *living one day at a time*. We in Al-Anon can, if we work at it, free ourselves from yesterday and tomorrow. Today is only one little set of 24 hours, a reasonably manageable bit of time that we can concentrate on using well.

Today's Reminder

I will not allow myself to be swamped by thoughts of things that are past. I will not concern myself about tomorrow until it becomes my today. The better I use today, the more likely it is that tomorrow will be bright.

> "Let not my thought fantasies lead me into anticipating trouble, since I cannot know what the future may bring."

How often we hear it said at meetings that the alcoholic is a past master in the art of conniving and manipulating us to get his own way and get out of difficulties. But do we realize that we ourselves have often been guilty of the same fault? Haven't we tried all sorts of tricks to outwit him—to make him stop drinking, to make him join AA, to make him go to *more* meetings, or go to *fewer* meetings? Am I being perfectly honest and fair when I meddle and manipulate our situation? Am I really letting the alcoholic live his own life, or am I still trying to be the boss?

Today's Reminder

Al-Anon principles set a pattern before me: to work on myself and to stop interfering with others. The words for this procedure are "hands off!"

> "Attending to my own business will
> keep me from becoming a slave to
> a situation; that is why I will
> not get myself involved too deeply.
> This will set me free to
> work out my own salvation."

Sometimes I find myself relapsing into the old patterns that used to dominate my thinking and feeling before I knew Al-Anon. I was crushed and defeated by the daily battering of living with an alcoholic. I was afraid of everything and everybody.

Then, by attending meetings, and reading *Al-Anon Faces Alcoholism,* my courage began to seep back into me. Yet sometimes, facing a new crisis or a challenge, such as being asked to speak at a meeting, all the old fears and doubts come surging back. But only for the moment. I remind myself of all I have learned in Al-Anon, and of the new dignity and confidence it has given me.

Today's Reminder

When I am able to accept the help of my Higher Power, it makes me feel capable of doing anything I am called upon to do. I am overcoming my fears. I am acquiring a comfortable new confidence.

> "Courage is fear that has said
> its prayers."

I will take a long and thoughtful look at the concept of *silence*. Used in times of reflection and meditation, it is a blessing. But it has other uses not so beneficent. We hear it said in Al-Anon meetings: "Try not to scold or reproach the alcoholic. Don't react with angry words to his guilt-laden ravings." This good counsel is sometimes misinterpreted. A member, thinking she has learned this lesson, will say with pride: "I kept my mouth shut. I didn't answer him." A grim and furious silence can be more crushing and wounding than harsh words. Such a silence is motivated by the desire to punish. It is the fruit of bitterness and resentment.

Today's Reminder

Silence can be a two-edged weapon. It will hurt me if I use it to hurt someone else. Silence can also be a blessing, if I enter into it serenely to take stock of myself and meditate on how I can improve.

> "God help me to know that silence,
> like speech, can reflect my inner
> feelings. Help me to use it, not
> as a cork to keep my anger bottled
> up, but to express a healing quiet
> of the spirit."

Why is it so hard to admit we are powerless over alcohol, as the First Step suggests we do? All of us have heard and shared in discussions, at Al-Anon meetings, as to whether this should be interpreted as "alcohol" or the "alcoholic." We have no power over either one. No one can control the insidious effect of alcohol, or its power to destroy the graces and decencies of life. No one can control the alcoholic's compulsion to drink. But we *do* have a power, derived from God, and that is the power to change our own lives. *Acceptance* does not mean submission to a degrading situation. It means accepting the fact of a situation, and then deciding what we will do about it.

Today's Reminder

Progress begins when we stop trying to control the uncontrollable, and when we go on to correct what we have the right to change. If we accept a situation full of misery and uncertainty, it is no one's fault but our own. We *can* do something about it!

> "Fighting futility is just a waste of
> energy, Samantha. Either do something
> or quit fretting."
>
> (Celebra Tueli)

At times I go to Al-Anon meetings in a captious, critical mood that I am not even aware of. By an odd coincidence, everybody happens to irritate me. This one talks too much—that one hasn't enough tolerance for others—another has said or done something I consider unkind. Could it be that *my* attitude is at fault? Let me go back to the Al-Anon fundamentals. What am I looking for? Help and enlightenment! Will I find it if I am only looking for flaws in others? I must remember that I am here for the sole purpose of improving myself and my way of life, and in every meeting there is some good to be gained, no matter what is said or done.

Today's Reminder

I will guard against looking for flaws in others; I will try to see what is good in them. I go to Al-Anon to learn, and every meeting is precious.

> "I have learned silence from the
> talkative; tolerance from the
> intolerant and kindness from the
> unkind. I should not be ungrateful
> to those teachers."
> (Kahlil Gibran: *Sand and Foam.*)

Our meetings generally open with a welcome which explains the purposes of our fellowship. It tells us we are there to share experience, strength and hope with each other. We are asked to share our *experiences* in applying the Al-Anon program to our lives. The *strength* we share with the others gives each of us a little more courage to face daily challenges. And, finally, we share our *hope* with each other so we may all be confident that there is a better life ahead for us.

Today's Reminder

Do I always consider the three elements of Al-Anon's togetherness before I speak? Or do I use the meeting time to complain about the alcoholic's faults? Do my words, my voice and my manner reveal my self-pity and resentment? Or do I try to bring my share of *good* things—experience, strength and hope—to my friends in Al-Anon?

> "I will not expect a whole meeting
> to give ear to my woes. I pray
> that what I bring to it will
> help and inspire others, or pose
> a problem on which we can all
> sharpen our understanding."

Having lived through more trouble than we felt we deserved, some of us turned our backs on God, determined to go our own way, under our own power. This is like a child who walks into a dark room and refuses to turn on the light. When he stumbles and hurts himself, is the darkness to blame? If we are going somewhere, and we reject the power of a train or a car to take us there, whose fault is it that our arrival is so long delayed?

When we are faced with the perplexities of the alcoholic situation, and try to do it on our own, we are stubbornly refusing the help that could be ours in Al-Anon. Whose fault is it, then, when things get worse instead of better?

Today's Reminder

When I am confronted with a problem, I will calmly search out the most intelligent means of solving it. I will use the means that have helped so many others with problems like mine. The Al-Anon program will be my daily guide, leading me out of confusion into serenity.

> "Unless I love my martyrdom and
> cling to it, I need not be alone
> in freeing myself from whatever
> troubles me."

My old enemy, self-will, used to masquerade
under rationalizations like this: "Why do I
need to lean on God and burden Him with my
problems when he has already given me the
intelligence to think for myself?" Experience
has taught me that I couldn't make any headway by relying on my own devices to bring
about the results I wanted. Nothing seemed to
work out; sometimes the results were disas-
trous. Of course I didn't blame myself! I
thought luck was against me, or God had let
me down, or the alcoholic was perversely unmanageable. Things just wouldn't go *my* way.
Now that I know I need guidance, and I am
willing to accept it, things are improving as I
improve.

Today's Reminder

I am not self-sufficient. I don't know all the
answers. The answers I get, in fact, come to me as
I keep myself receptive for them. Guidance comes
from the group, from something I chance to read,
and even from someone's word that providentially
meets my need.

> "God is our refuge and our strength,
> a very present help in trouble."

> (*Psalms*)

Oddly enough, many of the things we learn in Al-Anon add up to this: *"Be good to yourself."* That's the counsel to be drawn from Al-Anon's reminder to live only one day at a time. It teaches us to toss aside the unhappy memories of the past and to save ourselves the pain of imagining what will happen tomorrow. We can't do anything about either one. We are being good to ourselves when we refuse to be disturbed by anything the alcoholic says or does. We can do this if we remember that the attacks on us only give vent to his own agonizing guilt. We're being good to ourselves when we help others, and when we fill our lives with pleasant and rewarding activities.

Today's Reminder

Beginning today, right this minute, I will be good to myself. I will not allow myself to drown in the whirlpool of distressed thinking about alcoholism and its results. Confidence and hope will immunize me.

> "I pray for help to fulfill my
> responsibility to myself; only
> then can I help others."

The contented, well-adjusted person has no need to look for flaws in others. If in our thinking, one critical thought leads to another, the habit of making adverse judgments can grow into a major fault. Such criticism has the effect of pushing love right out of the picture. This, in turn, leads us to feeling sorry for ourselves because people do not respond to us as we would like them to.

I cannot change another person, and I have no right to try. What I can do is to change my own outlook on life, so I can see other people's good and pleasant qualities. I can do this by living the Al-Anon way.

Today's Reminder

With Al-Anon's help, I can make my battered old world into a shining new one. I have often seen it happen for many people I have met in Al-Anon. When I see such changes, I know they can happen to me, too.

> "I ask for the help of my Higher Power
> in making my little victories into bigger
> ones by living each day as well as I can,
> for myself and everyone I encounter."

The Al-Anon program really works because it helps us to *get away from ourselves*. When we think constantly about our grievances and the "faults" of the alcoholic, our minds are too confused to accept new ideas.

I will drop this fruitless worrying and concentrate on strengthening myself to accept each day along with whatever it brings. With my mind and my emotions refreshed and cooled by working one of the Twelve Steps or a slogan ("Let go and let God," for example) I will be better able to see my difficulties in their correct perspective.

Today's Reminder

As I become less *self*-centered, I will have stronger defenses against being hurt by slights and injustices. Minor crises will not loom large because I will not allow myself to magnify them out of proportion to their importance.

> "I pray that I may grow in my ability
> to use each day with poise, wisdom
> and a touch of humor. With God's help,
> I can teach myself not to turn little
> troubles into big ones."

It really isn't so hard to believe in miracles in Al-Anon. We see such miraculous changes in people who came as newcomers filled with self-pity and resentment and beset with fears. There may not even have been any improvement in their alcoholic situation at home, but what they learn in Al-Anon makes a tremendous difference in their own outlook. They gain confidence and poise, they come out of their shells and concern themselves with others in similar trouble.

All of this can be attributed to the sound spiritual sense that Al-Anon makes; but certainly "miracle" is a good word to describe the results.

Today's Reminder

The first gift a newcomer receives from contact with Al-Anon is *hope*. Seeing how others rise above their problems, listening to situations worse than their own, absorbing the atmosphere of love and good-will, sends them home with a new lease on life

> "Let me always be willing to lead a
> newcomer by the hand and bring to light
> the latent courage and confidence that
> exists in every one of us. Let me, in
> such sponsoring, help Al-Anon to produce
> still another miracle."

All of us know the maddening frustration of trying to reach the drinker when he or she is in the grip of an alcoholic fog. Neither reason nor tears nor scoldings can penetrate it.

It is witless to greet the sodden, guilt-ridden homecomer with a barrage of angry words. The alcoholic's reaction will be no more sane than ours at a time like that.

Would I go to a foreign country and expect people to understand my language? We make just as little sense to the drinker in the acute phase. We can't speak his language; the alcoholic can't understand ours.

Today's Reminder

To improve my seemingly hopeless situation, I will begin when things are most difficult. That's the big moment—NOT for action and headlong speech, but for inaction, and silence unclouded by sullenness and self-pity. That, indeed, is the moment to Let go and let God.

> "Many things must thou pass by with a deaf
> ear, and think rather of the things that
> are for thy peace. It is more profitable
> to tu_n away thine eyes from such things
> as displease thee than to be a slave to
> contention."
>
> (Thomas A'Kempis)

A member once said: "The Twelve Steps were designed for desperate people like us—as a short-cut to God. When we accept them and use them, we find they open the way to using our God-given abilities which we have allowed to lie dormant."

The Steps are like a medicine which many of us won't bother to take, although we know they can heal us of the sickness of despair, frustration, resentment and self-pity. Why is this? It may be we have a deep-rooted desire for martyrdom. Consciously we think we want help, but some dark and hidden sense of guilt makes us crave punishment more than we want relief from our ills.

Today's Reminder

No one really needs to suffer unhappiness and discontent, or be deprived of the good things of life. We can find the way out by daily study of The Twelve Steps. This wholesome spiritual philosophy will help us find our way into the light of a good life.

> "I pray for the willingness to accept
> the difficult discipline of the Twelve
> Steps. Living with such a guide makes
> life increasingly worthwhile."

For my own good I will go to Al-Anon meetings with an open mind, ready to receive and accept new ideas. For my own good I will apply these ideas to my own life.

If I go to meetings with a mind tightly closed, ready to criticize what I hear, it is as though I were to hold a teaspoon under Niagara Falls in an effort to get water for my thirst.

Every Al-Anon meeting has something important to give to the listener and the sharer. I must be willing to listen and share.

Today's Reminder

I will remember that I go to Al-Anon for the instruction and emotional support I cannot find elsewhere. I will get help from others who understand my distress; I will ask for their guidance as to my own shortcomings which I may find difficult to recognize. I know I need not accept everything everyone says, but the thinking process it engenders will set me on the right path.

> "I pray that I may always bring
> a healing helpful message to my
> fellow-members in Al-Anon, and
> I pray for the willingness to
> search out the good in what they
> say to me."

Someone says at an Al-Anon meeting: "But I must 'cover up' for the alcoholic; what would my neighbors and relatives think of me if I didn't?" Another admits that she must make excuses to the boss, lest the alcoholic lose his job. Another goes to work to help pay bills that should be the responsibility of the head of the household.

Can we really delude ourselves into believing that such stop-gaps will work? Do we imagine they will do anything but *prolong* the alcoholic agony, since we know the disease is progressive? We would do well to realize that the inevitable collapse may be far worse than if we had allowed him to face up to his own responsibilities and mistakes, free of our interference.

Today's Reminder

If I take no part in protecting the alcoholic from the consequences of his drinking, and *allow* disaster to overtake him, then the responsibility for what happens is not mine. I should not *create* a crisis to "bring the alcoholic to his senses"—but I must have the courage to keep hands off and let the crisis happen.

> "I pray God to help me understand that
> the alcoholic's fate is not in my hands.
> I will leave to Him whatever action is
> to be taken, and guard against interfering
> with the working out of His plan for us."

Would I stand on the seashore and, like King Canute of the ancient legend, try to command the tides? It is just as fruitless to try to control the alcoholic. Yet this is what I would be doing in attempting to force sobriety by my will-power.

I must honestly admit that I am not even able to control *my own* thoughts, words and actions. There is much room for improvement. My first obligation is to make a truly satisfying life for myself. To do this, I must work on my own shortcomings, get on better terms with myself and those around me.

Today's Reminder

I will devote myself to overcoming my flaws of character and controlling my impulsive words and actions. This will leave me no time to concern myself with remodeling the alcoholic.

Once I withdraw my interference and protection, the alcoholic may realize that sobriety must be a personal, individual problem which no one else can solve for him.

> "I pray for the wisdom to know that no other person's salvation depends upon me, but on himself and God."

Sometimes we find ourselves in a situation so difficult that it seems like a long-drawn-out crisis; we cannot solve it; there is no way to escape. Such a problem will occupy our thoughts continually—round and round it goes and the more we think about it, the more we are engulfed in despair.

This is the moment to recall a simple phrase, a slogan or a bit of philosophy, and to say it over and over until our minds are filled with it, replacing thoughts of the tormenting problem.

It might be the Serenity Prayer, or a thought like the one an Al-Anon member sent in to the Forum: "Thank you, God, I can now see that thorns have roses."

Today's Reminder

There is some good in even the darkest troubles that happen to me. I can acquire the knack of searching out the good, and concentrating on it. Much depends on meeting my problems head-on, calmly estimating their real character, refusing to exaggerate them, and then drowning them out with an inspiring thought.

> "Painful experiences come from the thorns that wound us; they make us forget they also have roses. Yet we cannot expect to enjoy life's color, beauty and fragrance, without accepting the thorny challenges and learning how to deal with them, as we do in Al-Anon."

What am I really searching for in my life? Interesting activities? To meet my obligations to my family and friends? To make myself into the kind of person I will enjoy living with?

I may not realize all of these ideals, but it's a joy to work toward them, watching myself grow, little by little.

One good way is to take a really searching inventory and examine my motives. I need to understand *why* I do what I do, and say what I say. This will help me realize the kind of person I really am, and give me constructive ideas for improving what I don't like about myself.

Today's Reminder

It is far easier to be honest with other people than with myself. All of us are hampered to some degree by our need to justify our actions and words. Admitting my faults, to myself, to God and another human being, as suggested by the Fifth of the Twelve Steps, will give me a glimpse of the wonderful person I *could* be.

"I will pray for self-fulfillment, and through
   conscious effort make some headway
   toward being at peace with myself,
   which is my ultimate goal,
   embracing all others."

Newcomers to Al-Anon often ask what makes the alcoholic drink. They seem more eager to know *why* than to learn why *they* allow another's compulsive drinking to affect them so destructively.

The causes of the drinker's desperate need for escape through alcohol aren't easily explained, even by the trained psychiatrist.

We must accept the fact that the alcoholic suffers from a sickness. The family may be able to help him to want sobriety, by changing its way of thinking and acting. In Al-Anon we learn how to conquer our *own* self-defeating attitudes.

Today's Reminder

What a blessed relief it is to be able to face our problems with confidence, hope and serenity. If we can recognize and admit our own shortcomings with increasing honesty, it opens the door to a new world for us, and often makes a seemingly miraculous change in the alcoholic as well.

"Let me free myself from the illusion that
I can do anything directly to conquer
the disease from which the alcoholic suffers.
I need not suffer from another's illness, if
only I am willing to accept help for myself.
This indirectly helps the alcoholic."

Despair—how many of us suffer from it! Yet we do not realize that it is purely the absence of faith. We cannot despair as long as we are willing to turn to God for help in our extremity. When we are troubled, and can't see a way out, it is only because we imagine that all solutions depend upon *us*. We must remind ourselves that our human wisdom and ingenuity have often failed to bring the hoped-for results.

Perhaps our too-heavy burdens have made us lose what faith we once had in a Power greater than ourselves. Perhaps faith was never a part of our lives and we are not convinced we need it.

In Al-Anon we discover that the reality and the efficacy of faith, as a force for good, can be demonstrated. When we let go of an overwhelming problem and let God handle it for us, we find that Divine Principle truly has a part in our lives.

Today's Reminder

A natural faith is indeed a gift, yet it is never denied to those who feel the need of something to cling to and are willing to reach out for it. When I consciously surrender my will to God's will, I see faith at work in my life.

> "I will take comfort in unwavering
> faith, for without it I am helpless
> and alone. . . ."

No wonder that both AA and Al-Anon stress the importance of living just one day at a time. How much precious thinking-time we waste, fretting over past mistakes and missed opportunities! How often our depressed imaginings betray us into speculating about "what's *going* to happen."

Yesterdays have no value except as experience, to be used in making today and the future more fruitful.

It may be difficult at first to discard these negative thinking habits. Yet it's a relief to find we *can* unload the burdens of the past, and anticipate, rather than dread, our tomorrows.

Today's Reminder

A valid "regret for the past" could be awareness that we have hurt someone. Such regrets for offenses to others may often be healed by doing them kindnesses whenever we are able. Regrets for missed opportunities, however, can be erased from our minds by trying to make wiser decisions from now on.

"I pray to be relieved of the compulsion to worry about the past, and that I may not let my pessimism paint black pictures of what may happen tomorrow.

"Keep in mind that we can live only in the present and that all the rest of life is either past or uncertain."

Why do some of us do better than others in grasping the Al-Anon program and using it to solve our problems? Those who benefit most have the courage to face their difficulties instead of hiding them in some dark corner of their minds, to set up a gnawing sickness of spirit.

Most of us *think* we know what our problem is; but do we really? One way to discover its real nature is to write it out in detail. Putting it into words on paper, where we can look at it and correct it as our attitudes change, can be most helpful in making us see it clearly.

This should not be a catalog of grievances against others, but an attempt to state the problem honestly. Thus we learn that not all the difficulties were created by someone else, but by *us*, too.

Today's Reminder

Listing the good and bad elements in my situation will give me new insight. I will begin correcting my problems by changing myself. I will never try to compel someone else to change, for that would help neither of us.

> "Knowing that only complete honesty
> will bring me to self-understanding, I
> pray that my Higher Power will help
> me guard against deceiving myself."

Are we justified in getting angry at a person in an alcoholic fog? We are not—if we have accepted the truth that alcoholism is a disease. Has an outburst of temper, with accusations and reproaches, ever improved the situation? Hasn't such action on our part only increased our own frustration?

It is true that such explosions do give momentary relief to our pent-up feelings, but once we realize that they only make matters worse, we can persuade ourselves to channel our forces into making a constructive decision. Any action of ours to *compel* the problem drinker to do anything is usually doomed to failure.

Today's Reminder

I will pause and think before I say anything, lest my anger turns back upon me and makes my difficulties even greater. I will know that well-timed silence can give me command of the situation as angry reproaches never can.

"Let all bitterness and wrath and anger and clamour and evil speaking be put away from you."

(*Ephesians*)

"A soft answer turneth away wrath but grievous words stir up anger."

(*Proverbs*)

When I can finally persuade myself to let go of a problem that has been tormenting me, solutions begin to unfold that I never dreamed were possible. This should convince me that my human understanding does have limits— that there are things I can't figure out by myself. Only then I will let go—and trust to a Higher Power for help.

Such an experience—seeing things happen that I did not bring to pass—should prove to me that another person's actions and fate are not in my hands. The sooner I accept this, the sooner good things will begin to unfold in my own life.

Today's Reminder

To "Let go and let God" is the way we find peace of mind. Our stubborn self-will can only hinder the working out of our problems. If I really want to be free to build a satisfying life for myself, I must first release the alcoholic from my efforts to direct and control.

"May I always keep in the forefront of my mind that I am not all-wise and all-powerful. Only God is that—and it is on Him that I must rely."

It has often been suggested that we adopt a favorite maxim or quotation to repeat when we want to tide ourselves over a difficult time. Many of us use the Serenity Prayer in this way. Others, trapped in a baffling dilemma or tempted to a rash decision, often say: "Not my will, but Thine be done."

What can we do when a dark depression weighs us down, and we can only think negatively about ourselves and others? Such painful, puny thinking will often yield to the grandeur of these words from the Psalms:

"When I consider Thy heavens, the work of Thy fingers, the moon and the stars which Thou hast ordained, what is man that Thou art mindful of him? For Thou hast made him a little lower than the angels and hast crowned him with glory and honor."

> "Let me realize myself and my fellow man
> as the crowning creation of God. For
> He Who made us all never meant any of
> His children to be unimportant."

A compulsive drinker can never be set free from his sickness by treating him with contempt. Yet isn't that what many of us do? When the drinker's dignity and quality are hidden under sodden incoherence or violence, it isn't easy to remember that this helpless creature is a child of God, hurt, sensitive, sick with guilt, in need of our compassion.

Difficult as it is, our own progress must begin with correcting our attitudes toward the alcoholic when he or she is in the acute stages of the illness.

Emotional crises happen, too, after the alcoholic has become sober. We owe it to ourselves to meet these in the same way as though actual drinking had caused the disturbance. Nothing constructive results from meeting anger with anger; nobody wins the battle in which control is lost.

Today's Reminder

Quiet poise can be acquired; and it does have a decided effect on the drinker, who, even in an alcoholic fog, senses a change in us. But even more important, relaxing saves wear and tear on our emotions and preserves our own dignity.

> "Let me turn my thoughts away from the torments of the troublesome moment, and think of Your ever-present help and support."

Once upon a time a despairing husband of an alcoholic joined an Al-Anon group. When he found that the other twelve members were women, he felt a little silly and decided his problem couldn't be like theirs, so he stayed away and kept on trying to solve it by using the same old weapons that had never worked.

Another man in a like situation was also a little shy of trying to identify with the problems of "a bunch of gals." But he quickly realized that Al-Anon was offering basic principles that really worked. So he brought a friend, and that friend brought another, and finally everyone gratefully realized that the men in the group gave it a stamina and workability it might never have had otherwise.

Al-Anon is for people—people who have a problem they want to solve by sharing their experiences, strength and hopes with other people. The more varied the experience, the greater the strength and hope.

No matter who you are, if someone in your life is fighting the battle of the bottle, Al-Anon has an answer for you.

> "Your wife's struggle to get free
> of the grip that alcoholism has
> on her will probably defy your
> imagination.
> "No matter how sincerely she
> tries to do something about it . . . she
> meets with the same inevitable
> failure . . ."
> (from the Al-Anon booklet: *What's Next?*)

I try to be grateful when others in my group suggest changes in my attitude toward this or that problem. "Detach from it," advises one. "Try to get a perspective on things," says another. "Don't say anything when you're angry"—"Keep the First Step in mind . . ."

This is good counsel, but mighty hard to put into practice when you're face-to-face with a crisis. So I will give myself another bit of advice: "Don't blame yourself when you fail; just keep trying. You know you're improving— your Al-Anon friends can see it, even if you're too close to the problems to be aware that you're growing. Everything you hear at meetings, every bit of Al-Anon reading, supports your efforts to do a little better next time."

Today's Reminder

The most helpful of all reminders is the old slogan *Easy Does It*. When I can't accomplish all I'd like to, when I'm confronted with reverses and nothing seems to work right, I'll just remember *Easy Does It*. Somehow it guides me into a less hectic frame of mind. Changing to a more comfortable rhythm smooths out the bumps.

> "When I'm trying too hard to change things,
> when I forget to let go—when I demand
> too much, too soon, of myself and others,
> I'll ask God to remind me that Easy Does It."

Very gradually, in Al-Anon, we come to see the inner meaning of its spiritual teachings. Many of them we have known from childhood, from parental guidance and religious training. Yet we find there has been a wide gap between what we learned, and how we apply it to our daily living.

In Al-Anon I discover two roadblocks that have kept me from seeing the value and comfort of the spiritual approach: *self-justification and self-righteousness*. The first gives a grim certainty that I'm always right; the second smothers me in the delusion that I'm better than other people—"holier than thou."

Today's Reminder

Al-Anon offers this effective magic in helping us overcome the damage due to self-justification and self-righteousness: *Examine your motives*. What answers would I give if I stop in the middle of such rationalizing and ask myself: "Why am I doing this? Is this justification really honest? Are these rational reasons for my action?"

"I pray for the progress that is possible when I am completely honest with myself. On that foundation I can build a good life."

"If thou be wise, thou shalt be wise for thyself. . . ."

(*Proverbs*)

"How can I both love and hate the alcoholic?"
is a question often asked in Al-Anon meetings.
Both are evidences of our personal concern for
someone; we neither love nor hate those in
whom we have no interest. In a sense, they are
two sides of the same coin; love has a chance
to flower in a shared life; hate is love twisted
and warped by disillusionment and despair.

If this really is one powerful basic emotion,
love can replace hate when I can bring myself
to nurture it with hope, and with faith in the
inherent goodness of another human being.

Today's Reminder

I want to recognize and appreciate the good and
lovable qualities of the alcoholic, and not hate him,
but the sickness from which he suffers. His
gradual awareness of my appreciation of him as a
person can rebuild his confidence and self-esteem
and create a desire for sobriety.

> "By love I do not mean natural tenderness,
> which is in people according to their
> constitution, but I see it as a larger
> principle of the soul, founded in reason
> and spiritual understanding, which makes
> us kind and gentle to all our fellow
> creatures as creations of God."
>
> (William Law)

Among the many weapons we use to castigate the alcoholic—or other people we disapprove of—is sarcasm. True, it relieves our pent-up feelings, and if our remarks are really pointed, gives us a certain satisfaction.

Repugnant as it is in itself, sarcasm becomes even more distasteful when we find it comes from the Greek verb "sarcazo," which means to tear flesh. It is that form of irony in which the speaker is motivated by scorn.

If I have ever used this weapon against the troubled drinker, I promise myself not to do it again. I have no right to scorn anyone, since I can never know what creates the need to behave as they do.

Today's Reminder

I will make an effort to blend gentleness with firmness, to add a note of harmony to my relations with others instead of tearing and destroying. I will realize that the wounds made by sarcasm are slow to heal, and may defer the longed-for improvement in my life.

> "A scorner seeketh wisdom and findeth
> it not. He that is slow to wrath is
> of great understanding."
>
> (Proverbs)

Coming into Al-Anon can be like stepping into a bright new world. I begin to realize that I really can change my life by doing away with my fear, bitterness and resentment. This means I must guard against judging others by *my* standards. It means examining and improving those standards and living up to them myself. If I am bitter, it is because I have allowed myself to blame others for my fate—blaming Fate, or the alcoholic, or God, for everything that has happened to me.

Yes, coming into Al-Anon and living with the program can give me a new view of my world, by helping me to see myself more clearly and accepting Al-Anon's suggestion to change myself instead of others.

Today's Reminder

I had never admitted to myself that I was wrong or at fault in anything that happened. It was something of a shock to learn that I am expected, as part of the Al-Anon program, to search out my own shortcomings. I must be honest with and about myself in order to start on the highroad to serenity. Will I be able to meet this challenge?

> "Because a thing seems difficult for
> you, do not think it is impossible for
> anyone to accomplish. But whatever is
> possible for another, believe that you,
> too, are capable of it."

> (Marcus Aurelius)

Only the alcoholic can set himself free from
the compulsion to drink. The non-alcoholic
cannot force him to want sobriety, although
many of us feel we should be able to correct a
situation that is causing us so much suffering.

Yet the more I try to force the issue, with
tears, reproaches and threats, the worse it gets.

Al-Anon can help me to cope with the situation in an entirely different way, by showing
me how to recognize and correct my *mistaken*
attempts to force a solution.

The same philosophy applies to the problems we face after the long-desired sobriety
has come to pass.

Today's Reminder

I am powerless over alcohol and its effects on
another person; I cannot make him sober, no more
than I can be responsible for his drinking. The
First Step tells me this, and it tells me, too, that I
must acknowledge that my life has become unmanageable. My first task is to manage my own
life, whether or not the alcoholic is still drinking.

> "Help me to find peace of mind within
> myself by uniting myself with God's
> power and guidance. That is the
> spiritual way out of my difficulties—
> the only sure way."

What's so wonderful about Al-Anon? That it helps us to see ourselves as we really are. Al-Anon is wonderful for those of us who want to know ourselves, who are brave enough to acknowledge our faults. It helps us to examine, with courage and honesty, our good and bad qualities. Al-Anon works for those who want to build on the good and whittle away at the bad, until, one by one, we get rid of the self-deceptions that have kept us from growing into the kind of people we want to be.

What do I want Al-Anon to do for me?

Today's Reminder

The Twelve Steps, the Slogans, the Serenity Prayer and the loving concern of other Al-Anon members—all these will help me if I am willing to cooperate. My share in the job of rehabilitating myself is to study and practice the program, to meditate and pray, to attend meetings and to help others to understand and live the Al-Anon way.

> "The people that walked in darkness
> have seen a great light; they that
> dwell in the land of the shadow . . .
> upon them shall the light shine."
>
> *(Isaiah)*

Surely it is cause for rejoicing to have the alcoholic find sobriety at last. Yet too many of us assume this means that the bluebird of happiness has taken up permanent residence in our home, and that all problems have vanished.

How this new-found sobriety will affect me will depend largely on how I adjust to it. Am I ready to withdraw from the dominant role I had while the alcoholic could not face family responsibilities? Will I welcome his dedication to AA, and his frequent attendance at meetings? Will I truly cooperate with this miracle by continuing to solve my own emotional problems in Al-Anon?

Today's Reminder

I know that the alcoholic is conquering the compulsion to drink and is growing, spiritually and emotionally. My role in our relationship must be to overcome my personal shortcomings, so we can grow spiritually together.

> "In a re-inventory, I found I could no
> longer blame the alcoholic in my life
> for my soul sickness, my restlessness
> and my feeling of inadequacy. I will
> accept my share of responsibility for
> our troubles, for I have learned, in
> Al-Anon, that many of them were rooted
> in my own imperfections."

Have I the courage to face up to the problems that alcoholism has brought into my life? Can I believe that my situation is *not* really hopeless, and that I am capable of improving it? Can I keep myself cheerful when everything seems to be leading me to despair?

The answers *could* be YES, if I refuse to accept the alcoholic's responsibilities and leave them to him, regardless of the consequences. I *could* overcome my hopelessness by opening my eyes to the troubles other people live with, so often much worse than mine. I *could* bring myself to a brighter view of life if I weren't always feeling sorry for myself; despair is often a mask for self-pity.

Today's Reminder

Three things I will practice every day from now on:

1) I will stop being a crutch for the alcoholic.
2) I will not let myself concentrate on the distressing features of my present existence, but will look for the good things in it.
3) I will remind myself that self-respect can relieve me of the need for pity, my own and others'.

". . . in quietness and in confidence
shall be our strength . . ."
(*Book of Common Prayer*)

A little meditation on the word *forgive* can throw some rather surprising light on our understanding of the word.

We are asked to forgive those who have injured us. Unless we have first judged and condemned them for what they did, there would be no reason for us to forgive them. Rather we would have to forgive ourselves for judging.

The Scripture says: "Judge not that ye be not judged." If we do judge—no matter how great the injury, or how premeditated—*we* are at fault. Following this train of thought to its logical conclusion, we see that we can forgive only ourselves. In doing so, we also forgive the person whose action we have resented.

Today's Reminder

"Thou shalt love they neighbor as thyself" tells me I must first make peace with myself before I can learn to love others. I must remind myself constantly that I can never know any other person's motives and conditioning; I must, for my own sake, accept them as they are. A large ingredient of that acceptance is loving tolerance.

> "Father forgive them, for they know not what they do." (*Luke*)

> "And forgive me for judging and retaliating. Help me to forgive myself; I know this is the first step toward spiritual security."

It is said that everything people do has a selfish motive. The members of AA freely admit theirs is a selfish program. So, too, is ours.

We know that offering Al-Anon to those who need it—who need its reassurance, comfort and personal concern—will make bigger, better people of us. This is actually *constructive* selfishness.

It is high time we changed our thinking about that much-maligned word. The highest form of selfishness is to give of ourselves so that we, in turn, may broaden our understanding and confidence. The richest rewards come from helping others with no thought of reward.

Today's Reminder

The greatest thing we learn from the Al-Anon program is that we cannot get unless we give. And this is equally true of all phases of life.

Those who are not willing to serve the group, who shy away from sharing themselves with those in need of help, are very apt to find themselves frustrated in solving their own problems.

> "There are those who have little
> and give it all. These are the
> believers in life and the bounty
> of life and their coffers are
> never empty."
>
> (Kahlil Gibran: *The Prophet*)

Al-Anon, like AA, is founded on a spiritual basis, on acknowledging our dependence on a Power greater than ourselves. The thousands of Al-Anon groups around the world have members of many faiths; our fellowship does not follow any single religious discipline.

We simply accept the idea that there is a Power which is more important than man's own individuality. We believe we cannot thrive without reliance on a Higher Power, and that we must follow the ethical standards of behavior basic in every spiritual philosophy. We can find peace of mind and real fulfillment only through devotion to something above and beyond ourselves.

Today's Reminder

Understanding my relationship to God will show me that humility is an essential element of faith, and true humility will remind me to *Live and Let Live*.

Faith in a Higher Power can also help me overcome my faults. If I believe in a Power greater than my own, it would be unreasonable for me to behave as though I were all-wise.

> "I pray for guidance from my Higher Power in everything I do. I know that many of my decisions could have been more wisely made, if I had been more receptive to His guidance."

Most of us in Al-Anon realize the importance of prayer. We may "think" a prayer
many times a day: ("Thank You, God, for
helping me to do this chore;" "Please let me
see the beauty in the ordinary and usual: a
tree, a child, a sunrise;" "Help me not to brood
on this injury but show me where I am at
fault,"—and so on.) We may pray night and
morning, asking for guidance to making
changes in our lives, or for light on a troubling
situation.

Prayer is simply a reaching out to make
contact with a Power greater than ourselves. It
is an acknowledgment of our personal helplessness, which has been demonstrated to us
so often in our efforts to find peace and security.

Today's Reminder

Prayer is the contact I make with God in my
thoughts. It is a powerful medicine for the spirit.
Prayers for guidance are perhaps the most potent
of all, providing I keep myself receptive, and am
willing to act according to His inspiration.

"All true prayer somehow confesses our
absolute dependence on God. It is
therefore a deep and vital contact with
Him . . . It is when we pray that we really
are."
                (Thomas Merton: *No Man Is an Island*)

This is a story about a man who has dedicated his life to helping the families of alcoholics.

On one occasion, he was invited to address an important Al-Anon meeting in a place about seven hundred miles from his home. Shortly before this event, he lost his beloved wife.

Those who had asked him to appear thought he would certainly not wish to keep his speaking engagement. But he did.

To one of the members who had expressed her sympathy he said: "Let me tell you a story of an Englishwoman at the time of the Blitz in the Second World War. Her husband had met sudden death, and her minister went to break the news to her. When she greeted him she asked: "Are you bringing me bad news that you come at this unusual time of day?" "I'm afraid so," the minister answered. "Is it about my husband? Is he dead?" "Yes, I am sorry to bring you such sad tidings . . ."

She interrupted him to say: "Come in and let me make you a cup of tea." At his astonished look, she explained, "My mother taught me, when I was a little girl, that when anything very dreadful happens, I must think of *what I would be doing if it had not happened, and then do that.*"

He gave a moving and inspiring talk to the assembled Al-Anons. Everyone marveled at his ability to rise above his personal sorrow, but few realized he had distilled that sorrow into inspiration for us.

In a sense, everything that happens to me is a gift from God. I may resent disappointments, rebel against a series of misfortunes which I regard as unmerited punishment. Yet in time I may come to understand that these can be considered gifts of enlightenment. They teach me that many of my punishments are self-inflicted. In some way unfathomable to my human intelligence, my suffering *could be* the consequence of my own attitudes, actions or neglects.

This spiritual approach to my problem can lift my thinking to a level at which I can gain new perspectives and find solutions I never dreamed were possible.

Today's Reminder

All of us tend to rebel against the unhappiness in our lives; we try to understand; we resent hat we cannot understand. Rebelliousness will only heap one frustration on another until we learn to get out from under, let go, and let God take a hand in our affairs.

> "When a man of good-will is troubled
> or tempted, or afflicted with evil thoughts,
> then he can better understand
> how great a need he has of faith in God."
> *(Thomas A'Kempis)*

I have much more to be grateful for than I realize. Too often I don't remember to give thought to all the things in my life that I could enjoy and appreciate.

Perhaps I don't take time for this important meditation because I'm too preoccupied with my woes. I allow my mind to keep filled with grievances, and the more I think of them, the bigger they loom. Instead of surrendering to God and His goodness, I let myself be controlled by the negative thinking into which my thoughts are apt to stray unless I guide them firmly into brighter paths.

Today's Reminder

A period of meditation, every day, is necessary to spiritual development. I control these "thinking times". If I meditate on what is good in my life, it will increase day by day and crowd out the self-pity and resentment over what I lack and what is hurting me. Suddenly I will find myself able to use God's help in managing my life in order and serenity.

"God has given us the faculties by which
  we are able to bear what comes to pass
  without being crushed or depressed thereby.
  Why then do we sit and moan and groan, blind
  to the Giver, making no acknowledgment to
  Him, but giving ourselves to complaints?"

                                        (*Epictetus*)

While we do not come to Al-Anon for the purpose of getting the alcoholic to stop drinking, it is true that membership in an Al-Anon group has been an important factor in many an alcoholic's recovery.

Nevertheless, our first concern is our own improvement. For this reason we do not discuss the actions and faults of our spouses, but confine ourselves to overcoming the tensions and anxieties of our own situations. We who are in the family circle of an alcoholic, suffer fears and frustrations; we feel beaten, hopeless and angry—with *overtones of guilt.*

Once we realize that alcoholism is a disease, and that *we are not responsible for it,* we can master our own feelings of guilt and hostility. This often brings about improvement in the home situation.

Today's Reminder

In our group discussions we avoid long recitals about the misbehavior of the alcoholic, because they do not promote our growth. We are in Al-Anon to get rid of our own feelings of guilt and hostility. We can deal more adequately with problems when heart and mind are not weighed down by negative emotions.

> ". . . then shall vanish all vain
> imaginings, all evil disturbances
> and superfluous cares."

Al-Anon's main purpose is to help those who are living in an alcoholic situation. To this end we share experience, strength and hope with each other.

What we don't do, and should not do, is to share one another's burdens, whether financial or emotional. Sometimes an over-eager member, impelled by a warm, friendly desire to help, will assume someone else's responsibilities—providing necessities, lending money or advising decisive or irrevocable action.

This is not helping. We help best by inspiring people to *think through and solve their own problems*. Otherwise we deprive them of the opportunity to develop experience and strength from working things out for themselves.

Today's Reminder

I need and want the inspiration and emotional support of those in my group, but I will not *lean* on anyone for help. I want to face my own problems and not sidestep them. Likewise I will not *interfere* with the life of anyone else, even though I am motivated only by a desire to help.

> "There is danger in taking on another's duty—danger that we may neglect our own, and that we may deprive them of what they may learn from finding their own solutions."

Among the many gifts we are offered in Al-Anon is freedom. When we are new in Al-Anon, we are prisoners of our own confusion and despair. Working with the program offers us release as we learn to understand the true nature of our situation. The gifts of Al-Anon are not without a price-tag; freedom for example, can only be achieved by paying the price we call *acceptance*. If we can accept the First Step, we are set free from the need to control the alcoholic. If we can surrender to God's guidance, it will cost us our self-will, so precious to us who have always thought we could dominate. It is up to us to decide whether freedom from our despair is worth all this. Most of us believe it is.

Today's Reminder

Success with the Al-Anon program demands that we think, honestly and in depth, about our attitudes, evaluating our words and actions. When the attitudes change from hostility to forgiveness, from violence to quiet acceptance, our words and actions follow along.

> "Freedom has many facets, but mostly
> it releases us from much that has
> been troubling and defeating us.
> We pray for this release into
> freedom."

When an Al-Anon wife describes her grievances at a meeting, and explains "what *she* did because of what *he* did," it is very possible that we can see through her motivations more clearly than she can. We see the bitterness, the self-pity and self-deception that have built a wall between her and reality. The suffering is real, but we wonder how much of the hurt is self-inflicted. It may be caused by the wife's stubborn refusal to let go of her control of the drinker. Or she may unknowingly distort and exaggerate what the alcoholic says and does.

Today's Reminder

I will examine, with a sharp and honest eye, my *own* motives, for I need to do a lot of straight thinking about my own attitudes and actions.

If I am troubled, worried, exasperated or frustrated, do I rationalize the situation and put the blame on someone else? Or can I honestly admit that I may be at fault? My peace of mind depends on overcoming my negative attitudes. I must try, day by day, to be honest with myself.

> "We blame little things in others and
> pass over great things in ourselves;
> we are quick enough in perceiving and
> weighing what we suffer from others,
> but we mind not what others suffer from
> us."
>
> (*Thomas A'Kempis*)

When we hear an Al-Anon member say "Detach from the problem," we react in various ways. We may think rebelliously: "How can they expect me to detach from my own wife or husband? Our lives are bound together and I am involved, whether I want to be or not."

That is true, but there are kinds of involvement that can only make our difficulties worse. We make trouble for ourselves when we interfere with the alcoholic's activities, trying to find out where he is, what he's been doing, where the money went. Suspicion, searching and prying will only keep us in a state of turmoil, and make the situation worse, instead of improving it.

Today's Reminder

What we are meant to know will come to our knowledge without any action on our part. This is a basic spiritual truth, implicit in our slogan, *Let go and let God.* When action is really required, as when a crisis happens, we will then be better prepared to meet the emergency.

> "He that is in perfect peace suspects
> no one, but he that is discontented and
> disturbed is tossed about with various
> suspicions; he is neither quiet himself,
> nor does he allow others to be quiet."
> *(Thomas A'Kempis)*

What is the greatest hindrance to my achieving serenity? *Determination*—the grim resolve that I can *do something* about everything. This whole feeling of tightening up, girding oneself for battle, can defeat my purpose. Over and over, in a hundred different ways, I learn in Al-Anon that I must let go. It will do nothing constructive for me if I retaliate for injuries I suffer because of the alcoholic. I am not empowered by God to even up scores, and make others "pay for what they did to me." I will learn to relax my stubborn grip on all the details of my sufferings, and allow the solutions to unfold by themselves.

Today's Reminder

I am only a small cog in the machinery of the universe; my trying to run things my own way is doomed to failure. A bright and serene success is at hand once I learn to let go. Then I'll have time to count my blessings, work on my own shortcomings, and enjoy each minute of every day.

> "What hurt could it do thee if thou wouldst let it pass and make no account of it? Could it even so much as pluck one hair from thy head?"
>
> (*Thomas A'Kempis*)

Perhaps the first thing we expect to learn in Al-Anon is how to get the alcoholic to stop drinking. This is a difficult idea to pry ourselves loose from, but our "making it" in Al-Anon depends entirely on realizing that our spouse's sobriety is not our business, however much it may seem to affect our lives and destroy our happiness.

The key figure in my Al-Anon work is I, me, myself. That's where the changes must take place to change my outlook from black to pink! Our work in Al-Anon, *with ourselves,* often results in the alcoholic's *wanting* sobriety and getting it. This is merely a lovely bonus for our dedication to the Al-Anon program.

Today's Reminder

I will stop wondering what to do about the alcoholic, and think about myself. What can I do to improve my life, to restore myself to full citizenship in the world? What are the shortcomings that are hampering me, and how can I rid myself of them? That is the crux of the Al-Anon program, and it really works.

> "God help me to accept my powerlessness over alcohol and its effects. I will direct my efforts to improving the one life over which I do have power, my own."

What finally impels the spouse of an alcoholic to look for help in Al-Anon? One large factor is the need for reassurance, to *know* that we're not responsible for the alcoholic's drinking. We know we are being "torn down," usually by the drinker's own guilt and self-reproach. This has left us without a shred of self-esteem. We come in as nobodies—and we desperately want to be somebody.

It isn't that we're looking for approval and praise from others, but that we want the inner confidence that we are adequate and worthy of respect. We need to learn that we have rights as individuals, no matter how grim the home situation may be.

Today's Reminder

The restoration of self-esteem is one of Al-Anon's prime functions. It doesn't encourage a big-ego view of ourselves, but in helping us to see ourselves as we really are, we learn to sort out our good qualities, and on that foundation to build stronger, better personalities.

> "I am grateful for what Al-Anon is doing
> for me. I am relieved to know that I can
> have a better picture of myself than I
> came in with, and that I must respect and
> like myself as a person before I can begin
> to grow."

A long-time friend of AA, Dr. Harry M. Tiebout, clarified brilliantly the difference between *submission,* and the *surrender* idea which is implied in Step One of the Twelve Steps.

"In submission," he said, "an individual accepts reality consciously but not unconsciously. He accepts as a practical fact that he cannot at the moment conquer reality, but lurking in his unconscious is the feeling: 'there'll come a day . . .' This is no real acceptance; the struggle is still going on. With this temporary yielding, tension continues. But when the ability to *accept* functions on the unconscious level as *surrender*, there is no residual battle; there is relaxation and freedom from strain and conflict."

Today's Reminder

Al-Anon tells me that complete acceptance of my powerlessness to change the alcoholic can, indeed, create a new life for me. When I really let go and stop playing God, things will begin to happen. Because at that point, my Higher Power has an opportunity to correct what seemed to me so hopeless.

> "Acceptance appears to be a state of
> mind in which the individual accepts,
> rather than rejects or resists; he is
> able to take things in, to go along
> with, to cooperate and be receptive."
> (*Dr. Harry M. Tiebout*)

"The hardest thing for me to learn," said a member at an Al-Anon meeting, "is to stop imagining that I can figure out why my husband acts the way he does. Automatically almost, I jump to conclusions about his activities and his motives. I know in my heart that I can't read his mind, and that anything I attribute to him is probably all wrong. Even his worst moments—the times when I'm exasperated to the point of fury—may just be his unhappiest. How can I know? Why do I judge?

"Nobody but God understands what goes on inside another human being. Let's not try to play God—or even psychiatrist!—to our troubled mates. Let's not examine them as we would a bug under a microscope. I always want to remember that every human being must be respected for his own individuality, no matter how battered it appears at times."

Today's Reminder

I will, today and from now on, examine my own role in all my confusion and despair. If I do this honestly, I will come to realize that I am not blameless, that there is much to be changed in me.

> "How can he think the way I think,
> Or do just what I'd do?
> (I will remember, day by day,
> My love, that I'm not you.")

In Al-Anon, we are encouraged to keep in touch with our fellow members between meetings. When I am depressed and apprehensive, it's a great help to call my sponsor or another group friend, and talk things over. But I want to be very clear on what I am looking for. Do I want comfort and a straightening-out of my thinking?

Or do I expect advice on a serious personal crisis? I cannot saddle someone else with the responsibility of telling me what to do. No one can make my decisions for me. That is my responsibility, and if it seems too heavy for me, I will call on my Higher Power for guidance. I will meditate and pray, and keep my mind open for the answer.

Today's Reminder

When I feel I must take a radical and irrevocable step, shouldn't I make sure I am not motivated by resentment, hatred, anger? I will remind myself that, once having taken a radical step, there is no turning back. Should I not try again, with the help of God and Al-Anon, to improve my own capacity for dealing with my problems?

> "Whatever faces me at this time, I
> know that God has given me the
> power to set my world in order."

When my body is sick, I take the medicine the doctor prescribes. When I am soul-sick and heart-sick, I need medicine just as much or more. Living with an alcoholic, and with my own neurotic response to that situation, I need the spiritual and emotional curatives that Al-Anon can give me. In the beginning I do not realize how much I need it, but when I see others healed of their despair, I find myself willing to accept this program.

People only deprive themselves when they blindly reject the continuing help of Al-Anon. Even when the alcoholic has found sobriety, they still need its spiritual support. They would profit greatly by "taking the medicine" until they can feel its beneficial effects.

Today's Reminder

If ever I found relief from my self-torment in Al-Anon; if ever I enjoyed moments of wonder at how much better I felt after being guided into this spiritual road to recovery, I will not lightly let go of Al-Anon. We all learn, sooner or later, that it can be applied to all facets of life, now and always.

> "It is comforting to know that I
> need never face my problems
> without the help of Al-Anon."

Once upon a time a woman came to Al-Anon to find out how to make her husband stop drinking. She was extremely well-informed about alcoholism; she'd read a lot of books. Now she was about to give Al-Anon a chance.

After six months of attendance at meetings, and reading all the Al-Anon literature, she could certainly talk wonderful Al-Anon, except that she wasn't really powerless over anything. She had her own way of using the program.

She went to AA open meetings and made friends. She introduced them to her husband (when he could navigate enough to go to a meeting with her). In time she built up quite a stable of sponsors for him. Every day she'd call somebody to remind him to call her husband, to come over and talk to him, or to take him to a closed meeting.

Her husband was dragged off to seven meetings a week. He agreed with everyone that AA was great. He was a mechanized puppet, powered by his wife's Determined Will. When it was discovered that she had set up a Great Big Multi-Sponsor Operation, the sponsors bowed out.

She wasn't powerless. Oh, no! But her husband kept on drinking. It was the only way the poor man could escape from the Terrible Domestic Powerhouse.

The newcomer to Al-Anon is looking for answers to a problem. The questions often begin with these two words: "WHAT IF . . ." *What if* we lose our home? *What if* he has an accident with the car? *What if* he stays out all night, loses his job, gets into fights, goes to jail? What if . . . ?

In Al-Anon we call this "projecting"—looking into the future and trying to imagine what may happen. The future—even as close as tomorrow—is a closed book. We cannot know what it holds, and the more we look for disaster, the more we invite it. Because the past has been unhappy is no index that the future will continue to be. This is something only God knows, and we would do well to trust in His loving wisdom and root out all our thoughts that "things can't get better."

Today's Reminder

It is health to the mind and body to look to the future with confidence. Lifting up our hearts is better preparation for disappointments, if they should come. Negative anticipating only increases the impact of unhappy incidents. Let's improve the outlook!

> " 'The thing that I have greatly feared
> has come upon me . . .' says the
> Bible. I will not give reality to
> trouble that may never come."

It is said in AA that the alcoholic who concentrates on the study and application of the Twelve Steps is bound to make good progress in the program.

This is just as true for us in Al-Anon. We, too, need to spend some time each day contemplating the marvelous light with which the Steps illuminate all our human problems. Neither alcoholic nor non-alcoholic limits his aspirations to sobriety alone; that is only the beginning. The Steps are a guide to total good living. As such, we would deprive ourselves of a precious boon in not realizing what they can do for us.

Today's Reminder

When I read a Step, and think about it deeply, I find it opens the door to new insights. When I read that same Step again, it again reveals new spiritual ideas. They seem to dig into our consciousness and unearth for us the wonderful potential for good in all our relationships with life.

> "If I had only half an hour of quiet time alone each day, I would devote it to studying the Twelve Steps so they would ultimately become an integral part of my thinking."

Sometimes an over-eager newcomer asks a number of people for advice about a problem, or is forever calling up various members to get their views on her troubles. For her there is one good piece of advice: "Get yourself *one* sponsor, and stop confusing yourself by trying to coordinate too many opinions."

She is trying to get all the answers at once, because she's in a hurry to put Al-Anon's magic to work. She assumes, of course, that she will be wise enough to sort out the right answer *for her,* from the welter of personal opinions, but her whole approach shows that she would be incapable of making a wise decision. She needs to go slow, let go, keep it simple.

Today's Reminder

Even when an Al-Anon member shows a confused or negative approach to the program, it can be a lesson to me. A single one of The Twelve Steps, a single Slogan, or the Serenity Prayer, used constantly, can clear my thinking and help me to solve my problem in the way that is right for me.

"Let not my thinking become confused by listening to too many opinions, but let me consider each one individually to see if it can be of help to me."

"To get a good, firm hold on the Al-Anon idea," said a speaker one evening, *"keep it simple!"* Because it *is* simple, and our slogans prove it. The whole purpose of Al-Anon is to help us iron out the rough spots in our living, and that can be done only *one day at a time*.

"Do you see what I'm trying to tell you?" he went on. "Those were two of our slogans, part of our Al-Anon therapy: *Keep It Simple* and *One Day at a Time*.

"Let's take a look at the others and notice how all of them are aimed at a relaxed approach. 'Away with grim determination, hurry and fretting,' says Al-Anon to her confused and struggle-weary members.

"Here are those great tension-relievers: *Let Go and Let God—Easy Does It—Live and Let Live—First Things First.*"

Today's Reminder

I will remind myself every day, and in all times of tension, to let go and relax. I will realize that, even in doing nothing about my problems, I am actively practicing the Al-Anon idea.

"Slow motion gets you there faster."
(*Attributed to Songwriter Hoagy Carmichael*)

The twelve simple words of the First Step embrace a whole philosophy of life. Books could be written on the subject of personal surrender suggested by the first six words: "Admitted we were powerless over alcohol." The next six represent our acknowledgment that we have not yet learned to handle our affairs wisely: ". . . that our lives have become unmanageable." The First Step prepares us for a new life, which we can achieve only by letting go of what we cannot control, and by undertaking, one day at a time, the monumental task of setting our world in order through a change in our own thinking.

Today's Reminder

I will apply the wisdom of the First Step not only to my relations with the alcoholic, but to all the people and happenings in my life. I will not attempt to manage or control what is clearly beyond my powers; I will dedicate myself to managing my own life, and only mine.

> "There's only one corner of the world
> you can be sure of improving and that
> is your own self."

The First Step tells me I am powerless over alcohol, which is admittedly stronger than I am, since there was no way for me to keep the drinker away from the bottle. It also suggests that the confusion arising from this helplessness has done things to my life that are not easy to endure. Then, going on to Step Two, I discover that the Twelve Steps are a closely-linked chain that will give me a clear understanding of my situation.

It says: "Came to believe that a Power greater than ourselves could restore us to sanity." This means that although we cannot help ourselves, there is help at hand. I am required to admit, also, that my own behavior was not sane. This is an invitation to humility, without which there can be no progress.

Today's Reminder

Surrender to a Higher Power, and the humility to make that surrender complete, is the first move we make toward relief from an intolerable condition. If I will do my part, I can rely on my Higher Power to open my eyes to solutions and restore me to peace and order.

> "Comfort and a peaceful heart are
> the rewards of those who rely on
> His help."

Why do I do what I do? Why did I say what I did? Why did I put off an urgent task? Questions like these, best asked of myself in a quiet time of meditation, demand honest answers. I may have to think deep for them. I must go past all the tempting self-justifications, the "reasons" that lack the shine of truth. I tell myself that self-deception can only damage me in giving me a foggy, unreal picture of the person I really am.

When I have given myself the answers, I will have made a good start in rooting out some of the shortcomings that block my search for serenity.

Today's Reminder

I can prepare myself to make decisions only by becoming aware of the kind of person I am, by getting acquainted with myself. I know I must acknowledge what is wrong, but I must also recognize my good qualities, for they are the foundation of growth.

> "To make good choices, I must
> develop a mature and prudent
> understanding of myself that
> will reveal to me my real
> motives and intentions."
> (*Paraphrased from Thomas Merton*
> *"No Man Is an Island"*)

We hear about the alcoholic having a "slip," returning suddenly to the bottle after a period of sobriety. We deplore it when it happens in our family, and most of us must confess that at this point we angrily blame the alcoholic for the lapse. If, however, I think of this as a "re-lapse," it will help to remind me that alcohol-ism is a disease that is not cured when sobriety takes over. I can no more blame the alcoholic than I would blame him for a relapse in any other disease.

I, too, have lapses from the Al-Anon pattern I have tried so hard to follow. When I fall into my old habits of self-pity and reproaching, my relapse is just as involuntary and forgivable as that of the alcoholic.

Today's Reminder

The bad moments will pass if I do not blow them up into tragedies. An old popular song says: "Pick yourself up, dust yourself off, start all over again." Al-Anon thinking can help me accept these shocks with equanimity and send me on my way to a better tomorrow.

> "I wonder if we non-alcoholics have
> ever realized that a relapse is a lot
> more painful to the alcoholic than
> it is to us. Let's not make it worse!"

Sometimes it seems to us we have more than a fair share of problems. We're so submerged in them that we can't imagine any way out. It's like trying to pull ourselves up by our bootstraps to raise our thoughts out of this frantic state.

We can do it, though, if we learn to use the leverage of God's help. It is always with us, ready to give us the lift we need. What happens then is that we are enabled *to see beyond what seems to be.* In Al-Anon, we call this getting a *perspective* on our troubles, instead of pin-pointing our thoughts on the trouble.

Today's Reminder

Whatever may happen today, I will think of it as a challenge which I am well able to meet. If it is good, I will receive it gratefully as a special gift. If it is not good, I will deal with it as well as I can, knowing it will pass if I do not let it overwhelm me. I will not let the good make me complacent, nor will I allow the not-good to drown me in despair.

> "Things cannot always go as you want
> them to. Accept disappointment
> quietly; cultivate the gift of
> silence when speaking may aggravate
> the difficulty."

The great danger of admitting resentment into our minds and hearts is that it often leads to retaliation. We feel justified in "evening up the score" and paying somebody back for what they have done to us.

But how can I logically punish someone for what he or she did to me when I cannot fathom their intentions or motives? Perhaps the hurt was not intended; perhaps we were over-sensitive. Or, as in the case of the alcoholic, most of us have suffered from unkindness. We have often been told in Al-Anon that the alcoholic's behavior toward the family is actually the backlash from his or her own guilt and self-hatred.

Today's Reminder

Nobody has given me the right to punish anyone, for anything; our Higher Power has reserved that right to Himself—"Vengeance is mine, saith the Lord." Therefore any attempt at retaliation for an injury can only react unhappily on me.

"In nature there are neither rewards
    nor punishments—there are consequences."
                            (*Robert G. Ingersoll*)

It isn't easy to grasp the Al-Anon idea of detachment. We are told to detach from the problem, but not from the suffering alcoholic. Yet when one disaster after another overtakes us, it is hard to distinguish between them.

Some try to do it by making a grim resolve not to speak. Such silence, filled with bitterness and anger, screams louder than words. It hurts us; it gives the alcoholic a cause for grievance, and it does nothing to communicate our love and compassion.

Others look for distractions to such a time-filling degree that their first duties are neglected, duties to the family and the home, including the alcoholic.

Today's Reminder

Detaching our minds from the problem can truly promote our spiritual growth, and lessen the unrecognized personal guilt we carry around within us. It can lift the mind away from the partner's doings. Such detachment shows us each new day as an opportunity to free ourselves from a sense of injury that is a blend of resentment and self-pity.

> "When I detach my mind from what
> is troubling me, my problems often
> solve themselves. Or it may be
> that leaving them to God gives Him
> a chance to take a hand in my affairs."

Sometimes, in an Al-Anon meeting, some-one makes a casual remark that reaches into my consciousness and takes hold. It comes to mind again and again because it gave me a new way of looking at things.

It might be a perfectly commonplace phrase, even a worn-out cliche that would have no significance *until it appears in a new context*. Then it springs into life and becomes a vital tool in understanding the Al-Anon program.

One member, explaining how she finally "got" the Al-Anon idea, said: "I just figured out that it all boils down to four words: *Mind Your Own Business.*"

An ill-natured phrase as commonly used, but as applied in Al-Anon, it makes great good sense.

Today's Reminder

I will concentrate on the things that are my concern—and make sure *which really are mine*. I will keep hands off the business of others. I will not interfere with the alcoholic's activities, assume his responsibilities or shield him from the consequences of what he does.

> "When you are offended at anyone's fault,
> turn to yourself and study your own fail-
> ings. By attending to them, you will
> forget your anger and learn to live wisely."
> *(Marcus Aurelius)*

The phrase "to create a crisis to make the alcoholic come to his senses" is often misunderstood and wrongly applied. It does *not* mean that we should interfere with the drinker's activities or plan pitfalls for him, or do anything that is *punishment* for the desperate sickness of alcoholism. Such actions cannot be excused on the ground that "it's for his own good." God did not give us the right to decide what is for anyone else's good; we would need His own Divine insight to know what drives the alcoholic to his frantic escape from reality.

Today's Reminder

No one *needs* to create a crisis for the alcoholic. He is heading toward the ultimate crisis every time alcohol takes control of him. Our role is to allow the inevitable consequences to overtake the unhappy drinker, as they surely will *if we keep ourselves from doing anything to prevent it*. The trouble that finally faces the alcoholic will be of his own making.

> "Scheming to outwit the addicted person is doomed to failure. Let's examine our own motives to be sure we're not playing self-defeating games. We will have to dig deep for this kind of honesty, but it's well worth it."

A member reminded a group one evening of a story in our book, AL-ANON FACES ALCOHOLISM, of the experiences of a commuter who talked with strangers each day on the trains, as she went to work. On every trip, she found someone with a problem of alcoholism: a young father taking his child to be cared for by his mother: an older man whose successful business finally went down the drain because of a drinking partner; a woman who at sixty had to take on the responsibility for grandchildren because both her son and his wife were alcoholics.

"These brief sketches proved one thing to me," the member said. "When we realize how prevalent the problem is, it's up to us to keep alert to help such people find Al-Anon. Every one of us could help somebody—a neighbor, a relative, a friend, or even a stranger. We need to do that kind of helping—it does so much for our own growth."

Today's Reminder

The Al-Anon program is a precious gift; I want to share it. I will not deprive myself of the opportunity of helping those who need it.

> "What I can give is never as much
> as I get from the giving."

In Al-Anon we hear many warnings against harboring resentment. It is a rare person who does not yield to resentment when he feels wronged by someone. Or we resent our fate, our bad luck, our lot in life.

No amount of self-discipline can heal us of resentment. Sometimes it seems the more we struggle against it, the more it sneaks up on us, surging like a dark sickness into the mind, plunging our emotions into turmoil.

We know it's destructive; we may earnestly want to free ourselves from it. What can we do?

First we think of our own personal good. Does it hurt the person we are resenting? Or does it hurt us? Then we reflect that this damaging emotion comes from *not understanding its cause*. Let's dissect it and find out what, inside us, made us react the way we did.

Today's Reminder

I have no room for resentment in my new Al-Anon way of life. I will not fight it with grim determination, but will reason it out of existence by calmly uncovering its cause.

An Al-Anon member wrote: "The best antidote for resentment is the continual practice of gratitude."

"Nothing on earth consumes a man more completely than the passion of resentment."

(*Friedrich Nietzsche*)

Philosophers, clear back to the ancient Greeks, have always made much of the idea of correcting bad habits by daily practice of good ones. In Al-Anon we make much of this, too. We learn we cannot go on functioning as we have been, impulsively and automatically, if we hope to improve our lives.

If we really do want peace of mind, the first thing to realize is that it *does not depend on conditions outside us,* but those inside us. An honest search of our own motives may show that we relish our martyrdom, or that we fear, subsconsciously, that we deserve it.

When we find the causes of our distress and frustration, we can establish corrective habits to overcome them.

Today's Reminder

A program of self-recognition and self-change "reads easy and does hard." Many failures come from trying to do too much too fast—and from expecting results overnight. I will search out just one fault, one bad habit, and work to eliminate that. As I observe the changes this effort brings about in my outside circumstances, I will find the courage to keep on changing myself for the better.

> "It is no easy thing for a principle to
> become a man's own unless each day he
> maintain it and work it out in his life."
> (*Epictetus*)

In Al-Anon we gradually come to realize the important influence that prayer has on our lives. The idea of prayer (how, why, when) calls for some reflection on our part.

If I were to pray: "*My* will be done," wouldn't it be exactly what I am saying when I ask God to do what I want? If I were to receive what I pray for, would it satisfy me and make me really happy? Do I always know what is best for me?

Prayer, then, is not the act of giving directions to God, but to ask to learn His will.

Today's Reminder

It should not be so hard for us to accept the obvious fact that few of us know what we really want, and none of us knows what is best for us. That knowledge remains in the hands of God. This is the best reason for limiting our prayers to requests for guidance, for an open mind to receive it, and for courage and confidence to use it.

> "I pray to be able to wait patiently
> for the knowledge of God's will for
> me."

"Nobody," said an Al-Anon member, "seems to give us credit for the courage it takes to live with an alcoholic."

Of course it takes courage, just as it takes courage to face life under any circumstances.

We need courage to believe that no situation is hopeless, to keep cheerful when we have cause for despair, to resist the impulse to complain to others about our sorry lot. It takes a lot of courage to resist the temptation to take over the alcoholic's responsibilities, until we accept the fact that we are only hindering his recovery by doing so.

Above all, it takes courage not to *appear* courageous as so many do, hoping for sympathy from relatives, friends and neighbors. "Poor brave little woman" may be food for the self-pitying ego, but it weakens character and destroys dignity.

Today's Reminder

Do I lack the confidence and the courage to do the things that will improve my situation? Am I afraid to let go of another person's obligations? Can I refrain from doing what can only hinder improvement? I may not have the necessary strength and confidence, but I can find them by turning to God and asking for His guidance.

"Prayers for courage and guidance never go unanswered. But I must be ready to act on that guidance."

"Now are come salvation and strength. . . ."
This phrase from the Bible was used by an Al-
Anon group as a meeting topic. Each member
told how he or she was "saved" from making
rash and perhaps tragic mistakes in dealing
with a problem of alcoholism, and how Al-
Anon's inspiration provided the strength to
meet the situation with poise and serenity—
and confidence in the outcome.

Most of us who have taken the program to
heart and really applied it to our lives have
had such experiences. But we must do the
work for ourselves, with constant reading,
meditation, prayer—and giving of ourselves to
help others.

Today's Reminder

The miracles I hear of in Al-Anon do not happen
to people unless they use their minds and hearts
to bring them about. Freely-shared experience,
strength and hope are at hand to save me from
discouragement and confusion. Do I want this
help? If I do, I will use a spiritual pattern of living for the solution of all my problems.

> "I soon learned, after a number of
> lapses, that Al-Anon didn't just
> mean an evening out, listening to
> a speaker, and forgetting the whole
> thing until the next meeting. It's
> an every day program that nobody
> else can work for me."

Suppose, in taking a break from my whirling thoughts, I settle down quietly to think about the word *"courtesy."* It means far more than mere politeness; you can be polite without an iota of personal love. Courtesy, on the other hand, is an expression of love, warm concern for the other person's comfort, peace of mind and well-being. Even giving directions to a confused stranger can be an act of courtesy, if I take the trouble to be explicit and reassuring.

The practice of courtesy in the home gives us many opportunities each day to convey our love in little ways. Yet we often overlook it in routine contacts with those we love.

Today's Reminder

I will take every opportunity to be courteous to those nearest me, as well as those outside my orbit. The warmth and kindness of courtesy will take the sting out of resentments, and give dignity and importance to the members of my household, making them feel secure and loved.

> "Courtesy makes a less troublesome game
> of life. Misunderstandings melt away;
> it gets rid of the avoidable obstructions."

What first brought me to Al-Anon? The promise of relief from an intolerable burden. I came, in other words, to *get* something, just as we all do. By and by I found that "getting" depends largely on my willingness to give—to be of service to others, whether it is just pitching in to help with setting up and cleaning up at meetings, or giving comfort and reassurance to others in trouble. The same spirit of giving must take place in every department of my life, particularly with those near to me. The name of this kind of giving is *love*.

Today's Reminder

Giving love is a fulfillment in itself. It must not matter to us whether it is returned or not. If I give it only to get a response on my terms, my love is cancelled out. If I have the capacity to give love, any return I get for it is a special bonus. It is through giving love, freely and without expectation of return, that we find ourselves, build ourselves spiritually.

> "Has a man gained anything who has
> received a hundred favors and
> rendered none? He is great who
> confers the most benefits."
(Ralph Waldo Emerson: *Essay on Compensation*)

What wonderful things could happen in my life if I could get rid of my natural impulse to justify my actions! Is honesty so deeply repressed under layers of guilt that I cannot release it to understand my motives? Being honest with ourselves isn't easy. It is difficult to search out why I had this or that impulse, and why I acted upon it. Nothing makes us feel so vulnerable as to give up the crutch of The Alibi.

Yet I know that self-deception multiplies my problems. How shall I correct this?

Today's Reminder

I will pick out just one character defect I can freely admit, and reason it away, right out of my whole being. Let's say I analyze my impulse to *resent*. If I convince myself of its futility, I will see unexpected, welcome changes in my experience.

I will examine my real reasons for every decision I make that *involves taking action*. If this shows me I am deceiving myself as to my true motives, I will try to correct this self-deception at its source.

"We know well enough how to excuse and color our own doings, but we find it difficult to accept those of others."

When a newcomer to Al-Anon tells his or
her sponsor about the alcoholic conflict in the
home, we must realize this is only one side of
the story.

At first these reports of our grievances are
highly-colored and dramatized by our confusions. A small incident may be blown up out of
all proportion to its reality; constant tension,
anger and frustration have deprived us of a
rational perspective.

Growth in Al-Anon brings us to compassionate understanding of the alcoholic's deep guilt
and unhappiness. As we apply the program
day by day, we become willing to acknowledge
that we, too, must share the responsibility for
the family troubles.

Today's Reminder

Al-Anon's challenge to me is this: deliberately
to cancel out my thoughts of grievances against
others, especially the alcoholic; to face the real
causes of much of my misery, and to believe that
I can do a great deal to improve my life by rooting
out my own shortcomings.

> "If you are pained by any external
> thing, look to yourself for release
> from it. When circumstances
> cause you to be disturbed, return
> to yourself quickly; do not remain
> out of tune with the Universal Good."

Our inspiring slogans mean such different things to different people! One woman, faced by a crisis, may say confidently: "I will let go and let God." In this case it is a courageous statement of faith that good must prevail, and that any decision she *might* have made, based solely on her human judgment, could have been unwise. She leaves the problem to God, expecting His guidance on what to do.

In another instance, *Let Go and Let God* may be a despairing statement of defeatism, an expression of apathy, of unwillingness to play one's role in the task at hand.

Those who simply turn their backs on their problems are not "letting go and letting God" —they are abandoning their commitment to act on God's inspiration and guidance. They do not ask for or expect help; they want the whole job done for them.

Today's Reminder

I cannot simply shrug off the responsibility for facing my problems, however great they may be. True, I need God's guidance, but acting upon it is my job; I cannot evade it without turning my back on life itself.

> "Let me not yield to apathy or
> defeatism, when in and all around
> me are the evidences of a loving
> God who will help me in all my need."

It is really a pity we cannot go to market and buy ourselves a big chunk of sense-of-humor, just as we would buy a package of yeast. They do about the same kind of job: yeast gives lightness and pleasant texture and taste to bread; the bit of humor works to lighten the heavy seriousness of our daily living, and smooths out the rough spots in our communication with each other.

Today's Reminder

I want to remember, every time I'm tempted to take a heavy, somber view of a happening, that it may not be so bad after all. Maybe, if I look closely, it has an element of fun—fantasy, absurdity or even a relieving silliness. My mood makes it look black when I could spark it with a dash of rosy pink.

I'll try to look for the things that can add gayety to my life, to offset the solemn or troubling ones. I'll cultivate a knack for recognizing and enjoying humorous moments. This could be a really constructive way of detaching my mind from my daily difficulties.

> "It is usually anxiety that bars
> us from seeing the lighter, brighter
> things of life. The anxiety exists
> within us, so we are free to reject
> its influence on the way we
> react to what happens to us."

An Al-Anon member of long standing writes of a tragic estrangement between her beloved grown daughter and herself. She had tried to prevent the girl from making what seemed to her a wrong decision, just as, years before, she had tried to compel her husband to stop drinking.

"Although I feared we would never be reconciled, I hoped I could find an answer in our program. I concentrated on the First Step: *my powerlessness over others.* What patience it took! What a constant temptation to take action, rather than leave the problem to God. But I made it—and it worked. The seemingly unyielding barrier of silence and, yes, hatred, melted away. We have learned again to love, by accepting each other as we are."

Today's Reminder

How often, in a crisis, we find it better to wait patiently for a problem to work itself out through a natural, inevitable process, than constantly to inject our own, perhaps misguided, control into it.

> "The beginning of love is to let those
> we love be perfectly themselves, and
> not to twist them to fit our own image.
> Otherwise we love only the reflection
> of ourselves we find in them."
> (Thomas Merton: *No Man Is an Island*)

If someone were to say to me: "Here is a medicine that can change your whole life for the better; it will put you in a state of relaxed serenity; help you overcome the nagging undercurrent of guilt for past errors, give you new insight into yourself and your spiritual value, and let you meet life's challenges with confidence and courage." Would I take it?

That is the promise of the Twelve Steps of AA and Al-Anon, if we do not cling to our burdens, our emotional upsets, family wrangling and wretchedness.

Today's Reminder

I will set aside a time each day to center my thoughts on the Twelve Steps. I will take them one at a time and observe how constant study changes my point of view.

It is no easy assignment, but life without them isn't easy either. My choice will be to take this beneficial medicine and let its healing magic work in me.

> "The Twelve Steps of AA which we try to
> follow are not easy. At first we may
> think some of them unnecessary, but if
> we are honest with ourselves, we will
> find that they all apply to us. . . ."
>   (*"Suggested Welcome" used at Al-Anon*
>   *meetings*)

When we come into Al-Anon, our main pre-occupation is the alcoholism of someone who is important in our lives. Step One says: "Admitted we were powerless over alcohol." We must sooner or later accept the fact that we have no way to stop the compulsion to drink. The desire for sobriety can come only from the alcoholic.

We may guide or inspire by our example, but we cannot cast another person, however close to us, into the mold that we choose.

The second part of Step One is easier to accept: ". . . our lives have become unmanageable." This we know. What we may not know, at this point, is what to do about it.

Today's Reminder

I understand that the First Step demands that I surrender the reins of control over other human beings. It reminds me that my life has become unmanageable; my first task is to set it in order. If I earnestly want to manage my life, I will have no time to manage anyone else's.

> "The First Step suggests a radical change
> in me—in my way of thinking about the
> alcoholic and my attitude toward him and
> his illness. Old destructive habit
> patterns must be replaced. . . ."

New people in Al-Anon react in various ways to the First Step. Most of them accept the idea of powerlessness, but only with reservations. They find it difficult to believe there is nothing they can do directly to compel the alcoholic to stop drinking.

Step Two immediately sounds the ringing note of hope. It assures us that help is at hand, the help of a Power beyond anything we can understand or imagine.

What can this Power do for me? It can "restore us to sanity." It can set my feet on firm ground and show me the way to renew my life which now may be too troubled to allow me to think straight.

My despair may have been so great that I had lost the faith I once had—the complete, surrendering faith in something beyond myself.

Today's Reminder

In my great need of comfort and reassurance, the Second Step suggests I surrender my will to the wisdom of a loving God in my effort to find a sane and reasonable way of life.

> "A little consideration of what takes
> place around us every day, would show us
> that a higher law than that of our
> will, regulates events; that our painful
> experiences are not necessary. A believing
> love will relieve us of a vast load of care.
> Oh, my brothers, God exists!"
>
> (Ralph Waldo Emerson)

By the time we reach our study of Step Three, we begin to get a sensation of gently, gradually, being led to truths we never realized or put to use.

This Step is a challenge to each of us, personally. It suggests a decision: to let go and let God take a hand in our affairs, which He can do only if we surrender our self-will and turn our lives over to His care.

Step Three is a distillation of the central thought of philosophers through the centuries. Wouldn't it be wise to accept their wisdom as greater than my own?

Today's Reminder

The words, "Made a decision to turn our will and our lives over to the care of God as we understood Him", could make life so easy for me, if only I could subordinate my will to His. This is a stumbling block for so many of us: we feel obliged to apply the force of our will to our problems. No solutions can be found in this way.

> "There is guidance for each of us, and by
> lowly listening, we shall hear the right
> word. Certainly there is a right for you
> that needs no choice on your part. Place
> yourself in the middle of the stream of
> power and wisdom which flows into your
> life. Then, without effort, you are
> impelled to truth and to perfect content-
> ment."

(Ralph Waldo Emerson)

The Greek philosopher Socrates said: *"Know Thyself."* Step Four tells us how to go about it, making "a searching and fearless moral inventory of ourselves." We are to see ourselves as we really are—our characters, motives, attitudes and actions.

A deeply rooted habit of self-justification may tempt me to explain away each fault as I uncover it. Will I blame others for what I do on the ground that I am compelled to react to their wrongdoing?

It has been said that even a trained psychiatrist cannot analyze himself because of such blocks. This will challenge me to prove that personal honesty and humility can achieve what superior knowledge often cannot.

Today's Reminder

A total inventory of my good and bad qualities can be interesting and useful as a start on my work with Step Four. But when I am ready to dig in and correct my shortcomings, I will work on only one or two at a time, and for as long as it takes to satisfy me that I have made real progress in erasing them.

> "Perfection is a long way off, but
> improvement can be made to happen
> every day."

The self-searching suggested by Step Four is a long-term undertaking. It must go on for as long as I remain blind to the flaws which create so much trouble for me.

I must go on day after day trying to face myself as I am, and to correct whatever is keeping me from growing into the person I want to be.

As I review each day and think over the consequences of what I have said and done, I can go on to Step Five, which suggests that *I admit these shortcomings, first to God as to myself, in a kind of private confession.* When that is done, I need the courage to complete the Step by confiding my faults to another trusted human being. Such acknowledgment requires both humility and honesty.

Today's Reminder

As I understand the difficult task of facing myself and my faults, I will guard against self-justification and self-righteousness. I am well aware how easy it is to make excuses for myself, and to blame my misfortunes on others, and particularly on the alcoholic.

> "To overcome my faults, I must first
> know what they are. Then I must admit
> to them, and, finally, with patient self-
> correction, diminish them, even if I
> cannot set myself wholly free."

The Sixth Step is an inspiring challenge to surrender ourselves to the guidance of our Higher Power. I will read this serenely beautiful statement of submission to God's will as often as I have need of it: "Were entirely ready to have God remove all these defects of character."

My goal will be to make myself "entirely ready"—to let go of the negative habits of thought that have been reflected in the happenings of my life. God is just as "entirely ready" to accept this humble offering of my faults, and to help me change to the kind of thinking and doing that will bring me serenity, and even, perhaps, happiness.

Today's Reminder

The "defects of character" I want to be rid of, are sure to have deep roots in habit. My daily conscious cooperation will be needed as I accept God's help in removing them. I will try to deal with them patiently, one by one. If I am truly willing, I will see them replaced gradually by impulses of a different quality, that I can live with, comfortably free from self-reproach.

"God make me entirely ready for the removal of my faults, that I may receive light on my problems and their true causes."

When my meditations on Steps Four, Five and Six have convinced me I am ready to be delivered from a hampering defect of character, the next Step, number Seven, suggests asking God to remove it.

Step Seven, as it is stated, does imply removal of *all* my shortcomings, but I must deal with *each one individually,* as I express it in my daily activities. I must ask God, over and over again, to release me from it.

Today's Reminder

I will not expect too much of myself, nor expect to accomplish my improvement all at once, nor without the help of my Higher Power. I must keep reminding myself to accept His help in all I am trying to do.

If, for instance, I concentrate on being tolerant and kind at all times, with everyone, it will soon become an automatic reaction, no matter how trying the circumstances may be. This new attitude will color whatever I do and make me more acceptable, to myself as well as to others.

> "Humbly asked him to remove our short-
> comings." (The first word is the key
> to Step Seven.)

Today I will consider, quietly and deeply, Step Eight: *"Made a list of all persons we had harmed, and became willing to make amends to them all."*

The central thought is *willingness*—to admit our errors so we can clear our inner consciousness of guilt.

The only action this Step calls for is to *make a list.* I can do this by allowing my oppressive, nagging guilts to rise to the surface of my mind, ready to be disposed of, so they can trouble me no more.

Today's Reminder

Whom have I injured? Surely those closest to me—my family. I know that my hostile reaction to the alcoholic has been hurtful. Have I also damaged my children by subtly indoctrinating them with contempt for their alcoholic parent? Have I communicated my anxiety and resentment to them? Have I taken out my frustrations on them?

> "The Eighth Step places us on the
> threshold of freedom from self-hate;
> it opens the door to new peace of mind
> which, once enjoyed, we will never want
> to lose."

What is to be done with the list of those we have harmed, as suggested in the Eighth Step? The Ninth suggests we make amends, "whenever possible, except when to do so would injure them or others."

Prudent and honest self-searching will be necessary.

A casual apology, for example, is rarely enough to get rid of guilt for damaging criticism. It may, indeed, reopen an old wound. A change of attitude can do much more to make up for past unkindnesses.

If I have deprived anyone of any material thing, I will acknowledge the debt and pay it in full.

Rifts between me and my relatives or former friends can often be healed by swallowing my pride and making the first overtures toward reconciliation. Even if only a little of the blame was mine, the generous gesture will benefit me.

Today's Reminder

Step Nine, taken with care and prudent judgment, will relieve me of a burden I have no need to carry.

"Love and patience can make ample amends
for past injuries; they restore us to
sanity and our lives to serenity."

In the Steps which precede the Tenth, we have been dealing with the past—cleaning house, so to speak. We have searched the corners of memory for grievances to be adjusted by means of our new view of our role in life. Now, with Step Ten, this procedure becomes a daily ritual, a housecleaning that takes place in a nightly review of the day's happenings.

"Continued to take personal inventory, and when we were wrong, promptly admitted it."

If this Step becomes a part of our daily life, there will be no backlog of guilt to worry about; we keep order as we go along.

Today's Reminder

The Tenth Step is essential to the Al-Anon promise I make to myself to live one day at a time. Although I cannot expect to achieve perfection, I can observe my progress and enjoy the deep satisfactions it can bring me. It may have little obvious effect on my outward circumstances at first but keeping myself receptive to solutions will guide me to them.

> "Look to yourself—it is there that
> all your answers are found."

It is in Step Eleven that I find the actively-spiritual prescription for the practice of the Al-Anon program:

"Sought through prayer and meditation to improve our conscious contact with God as we understood Him, praying only for knowledge of His will for us and the power to carry that out."

If we are living by the Al-Anon counsel *First Things First*, prayer and meditation come before all else, since it is in this way that we receive guidance for our decisions.

Today's Reminder

Am I too busy to pray? Have I no time for meditation? Then let me ask myself whether I have been able to solve my problems without help. As I face them day by day, I want to acknowledge my need for His guidance. I will not let this day pass —nor any day from now on—without making myself consciously aware of God.

> "It is God that girdeth me with strength
> and maketh my way perfect."
>
> *(Psalms)*

The final triumphant statement of spirituality which is announced in Step Twelve can come to every one of us as we live the Al-Anon way. *"Having had a spiritual awakening as the result of these Steps, we tried to carry this message to others, and to practice these principles in all our affairs."*

The spiritual awakening is a realization that we are not alone and helpless; we have learned certain truths which we are now able to carry to others in order to help them.

Today's Reminder

I will keep myself ready for the spiritual awakening which is certain to come to me when I have surrendered my will to God's will. It will throw new light on many things. It will give me the ability to make my judgments and decisions on the spiritual level where I will be governed by God's goodness and wisdom.

> "We are asleep; we walk in darkness
> until we find God's hand to lead
> us into His way—the way of spiritual
> enlightenment."

We who really try to use the Al-Anon program have various reasons to be grateful as we see the results. This was one member's experience, which she told her friends at a meeting.

Her greatest difficulty concerned her children. "I never knew what to do about them when my husband came home drunk and disorderly. I felt they should be shielded from violence, yet over-protection wouldn't be good for them. I didn't want to influence them against their father; I knew he loved them, and they him.

"I found all the answers in Al-Anon. I made sensible explanations about their father's illness and found them naturally compassionate. I avoided scenes by not allowing my frustrations to erupt into anger. I tried hard to be consistent and fair to them. The results have been everything I hoped for, and I am so grateful to Al-Anon for this."

Today's Reminder

Our children are a *first thing* to consider *first*. Our attitude is the key to a successful family relationship—and their normal growing up.

> "And above all, I never use the
> children as pawns in any conflicts.
> They respond so well to respect."

Among the many things we learn in our contact with the Al-Anon fellowship is this: *Be Good to Yourself.*

This is a surprisingly hard assignment for many of us. Some relish their sufferings so much that everything that happens is ballooned to enormous proportions in the re-living and the telling. Self-pitiers are difficult to wean away from their martyrdom until the joys of serenity and contentment dawn on them in Al-Anon.

Others nurse their grievances, resent their lot in life, seek scapegoats to blame for everything that happens to them, particularly the alcoholic. They have not yet learned to be good to themselves. They still have before them the joyous experience of letting go of a problem— the lovely adventure of shrugging off "hurts."

Today's Reminder

Very little that happens in my daily encounters is worth my worry, resentment, or feeling sorry for myself. If I am always ready to take offense and be hurt, I'm selling my contentment very cheaply. I must remember to be good to myself!

> "How happy and useful I could be if I weren't carrying around such a load of unpleasant emotional turmoil. No one asks me to, so why do I?"

We share with the alcoholic one common
enemy: *self-deception.* The recital of a troubled Al-Anon prospect may be full of gruesome
details of suffering; the story told by the alcoholic spouse may be equally harrowing, and
to those who hear both sides it seems they are
describing totally different relationships.

Each reacts in his and her own way to what
is happening. Each unconsciously suppresses
facts that might reflect badly on him and her,
and exaggerates the other's faults. Although
the situation may sound unendurable, it appears that neither has any intention of getting
away from it! Neither is in any state of mind
to see it rationally until there is a change of
attitude.

Today's Reminder

I will avoid making judgments in private con-
tentions; there is self-deception on both sides
which I cannot evaluate. I will guard against advising anyone to take a radical step he or she is
not emotionally ready to take.

> "Let Go and Let God is a good rule to
> follow when we are asked to give advice
> in a troubled domestic situation."

The time I spend in reviewing the past, mourning over past mistakes and failures, is time lost.

This is why the twenty-four hour concept, both in AA and Al-Anon, is so strongly emphasized.

Our yesterdays have no importance except as experience in making today more fruitful. Regrets and self-condemnation for what we did or left undone, only destroy the self-esteem we could derive from a *balanced* view of ourselves.

Today's Reminder

Regrets for hurtful things I have done to others may be healed by making amends as well as I can. Regrets for missed opportunities will vanish as I try to make wise choices today. Let me fill this one day with thoughts and actions I will have no need to regret. Let me undertake only as much as I can accomplish well, without haste or tension.

> "Just for today I will live through
> this one day only and not tackle all
> my problems at once. Those of the
> past need not concern me today; future
> ones can be faced as they arise."
> *(From Al-Anon's "Just for Today.")*

"This I learned in Al-Anon," says a member at a meeting, "that the man I married cannot be the source of my happiness or sorrow. The gift of life is personally mine—as his life belongs to him—to enjoy or destroy, as each of us wishes.

"I see him angry. Must I be? He is hostile. Must I be? Am I being faithless to my marriage vows when I achieve a bit of self-confidence while he continues to suffer the pains of self-doubt?

"I am not his guide, master or keeper. We are individuals and must each find our lonely way to our goals. My sources of comfort and strength he refuses to share with me; I have learned through bitter experience that it is fruitless to offer them."

Today's Reminder

Adjusting myself to things as they are, and being able to love without trying to interfere with or control anyone else, however close to me—that is what I search for and can find in Al-Anon. The learning is sometimes painful; the reward is life itself—rich, full and serene.

> "If thou attend to thyself and to God,
> thou wilt be little moved by what thou
> perceivest outside thee."
>
> (*Thomas A'Kempis*)

Some people I meet in Al-Anon seem to have a kind of natural joy-of-living. Their optimism tells you they know there's something good waiting for them right around the corner. Their hopeful confidence rubs off on every troubled person they talk to. They make every meeting a kind of special adventure.

Newer members are astonished to learn that many of these people, when they were new in Al-Anon, were also burdened with woe and black despair. It was Al-Anon that brought the joy-of-living, hope and confidence, out into the open, ready to be used to help others.

Today's Reminder

As soon as I am willing to dig into the program and put the Twelve Steps and the slogans to work, by daily reading and constant application, I will forget to be "mad" at people, forget to be sorry for myself. And that leaves a world of room and think-time for serenity, acceptance and gratitude for what is good in every day.

> "I'll only be able to help others when
> I have allowed Al-Anon to clear up
> my own view of my problems. Until I
> am impelled to share with others what
> I get from this program, my own progress
> will be limited."

Somebody once said: "The only difference between stumbling blocks and stepping stones is in how you use them."

It's a comforting thought that nobody can put stumbling blocks in my way, because I'm learning how to use them to step on as I progress to a saner way of living.

There's no discounting the troubles caused by alcoholism—they're big and terrifying. But I *can* refuse to let them block my path. I can imagine that each is one of the Twelve Steps. At least I have God's gift of sobriety to help me, unlike the sick alcoholic who is tripped up again and again by a built-in stumbling block!

Today's Reminder

Obstacles cannot keep me from finding the good in my life and following where it leads. Nothing can get in the way of this—unless I allow it.

Al-Anon invites me to take this action: to change my view of myself and the world I am creating around me.

> ". . . men may rise on stepping-stones
>   Of their dead selves to higher things."
>   (Tennyson: *"In Memoriam"*)

The poet Henley, in his challenging poem called Invictus, says: "I am the master of my fate, I am the captain of my soul."

The first thing I notice is that he speaks of *"my* fate," *"my* soul." If I have been behaving as though I were captain and master of anyone else, wouldn't it be a good idea to turn my attention to managing myself?

I must also recognize, however, that my fate, and the state of my soul, doesn't depend on me alone; I need the help of God to meet life's challenges. No human wisdom is adequate to make life wholly satisfying and successful.

Today's Reminder

God will take a hand in my life if I ask for His guidance, and keep myself receptive to indications of His will for me. Before Al-Anon I took too much on myself in trying to engineer solutions. Now I know I can only make right decisions by referring my problems to Him. God must be part of my life; I will "acknowledge Him in all my ways". Then it will be possible to rise above my difficulties.

"God dwells wherever man lets Him in."
(Martin Buber)

An AA speaker at an Al-Anon meeting gave the members this unusual insight from the other side of the fence:

"The non-alcoholic in the family doesn't seem to realize that the alcoholic is in a terribly vulnerable position. He must be constantly on guard, because he knows, deep down inside, how much trouble he is bringing to the family. He knows he is wide open to criticism.

"But did it ever occur to you that your tantrums and harsh words are like whipping a sick dog? Remember, he's lashing himself—all the time. If you apply more lashes, you're inviting him to transfer some of his guilt to you. This can keep him from reaching his 'bottom' and realizing how much he needs help to find sobriety."

Today's Reminder

I will try to understand how desperately the alcoholic suffers from guilt. I will not yield to the impulse to kick him when he is down. We both suffer in different ways from the alcoholism. I, who have God's gift of sobriety, must be the one to realize his dissatisfaction with himself, no matter how defiant and defensive he may appear.

"If I were unfortunate enough to be an alcoholic, how would I hope to be treated by the person I live with? The Golden Rule is a useful tool in all our personal relationships."

The change from active alcoholism to sobriety makes a great upheaval in our lives. It is
a challenge to both partners. Making this difficult adjustment requires entirely new thinking
patterns.

In the years of active drinking, the husbands
of compulsive drinkers had to take on many
extra responsibilities. Along with earning a
living for the family, they had to provide for
the care of the children, take care of the
home and get the meals. Wives of compulsive
drinkers often had to work to supplement the
skimpy budget, or do without many necessities, as well as doing the man's chores around
the house.

With sobriety, many of these roles must be
reversed, many habits unlearned. The Al-Anon
program, applied each day, will help us make
the adjustment to a normal way of life.

Today's Reminder

I will learn not to expect too much too soon, and
above all, not to expect that sobriety will transform
my spouse into a super-perfect human being,
tailored to my specifications.

Al-Anon will help to restore me to a sane and
reasonable way of thinking so I can deal with my
family relationships with love and understanding.

> "No great improvements are possible in
> the lot of mankind until a change takes
> place in their modes of thought."

What's so important about being right? Why do we complicate our lives and aggravate our difficulties by insisting that our views be accepted?

In the tensions that are part of living with an alcoholic, this attitude can make much trouble for us. What harm would it do to "back down"—to accept what the alcoholic says, whether it makes sense or not? Why don't I just Let Go and Let God?

I will try to apply Easy Does It to every incident that might increase the tension and cause an explosion. I will try to realize that an exchange of hostile words will not help me to find the serenity I want.

Today's Reminder

Why should I react to criticism and accusation, justified or not? What can I gain by heated denials and irrational discussions? In a neurotic environment, *anything* can start a row. I need not take part in it; I will ignore it—cheerfully if I can. This is an excellent technique for avoiding dissension. Our calm unconcern may make the alcoholic uneasy enough to make him think seriously about finding sobriety.

> "To withdraw from an argument may not make you the winner, but what you have saved is your own dignity and grace."

It is an interesting experiment, and an enlightening one, to listen to the *voices* at an Al-Anon meeting—not so much *what* they're saying, but *how*. The very sound and inflection can reveal the speakers' hidden attitudes.

What does the discerning listener hear in such an experiment?

In those who are studying the program and enjoying the fruits of *living* it, the tone and manner of speaking show confidence, humility, compassion for those in trouble, and an honest acknowledgment that they are not master-minds to solve all problems.

In those who are still bound to their unhappiness, we hear, beyond their words, angry judgments of the alcoholic, self-pity, and a grim determination to "win the battle," no matter what.

Today's Reminder

The way I speak often reveals more than what I say.

To make the program work for me, it is important to be *living it*. This will reveal itself in everything I do and say.

> "By listening to more than mere
> words I can learn much more than
> mere words can teach."

What kind of stuff is self-pity made of, that it can entrench itself in my mind and keep me miserable? It may be envy of those who have more of the material things—a better house, a finer car. It could be my resentment of monotony, not having enough relief from the daily grind. It may be because I am critical of others: "Why can't he do it *my* way; why did she say or do this or that?" Or bitterness because we're lonely if the spouse has merely switched from nightly sessions at a bar to nightly AA meetings.

Self-pity comes from concentrating on the negative aspects of life.

I will find ways to make my life more interesting, take a fresh view of the pleasant things that happen each day. I will work toward a more *mature* attitude—and settle for a little less than my romantic dreams make me think I ought to have.

Today's Reminder

An Al-Anon meeting is a great place to observe how various people react to their circumstances. Those who have the most to be grateful for often grumble and complain. Others, living desperate and even tragic lives, somehow keep cheerful and manage to get some joy out of what little they do have.

> "To expect life to be tailored to our specifications is to invite frustration."

When I am much troubled, I often find that the counsel of the cheerful optimist only makes my exasperation worse! I feel my sufferings aren't properly understood—people can't even begin to appreciate what a martyr I am! I think to myself: "It's easy enough to talk, but how can I smile when there's nothing to be happy about?"

Oddly enough, I have found that a deliberate effort to "laugh it off" does have the most astonishing results in shrinking my woes down to bearable size.

This is the helpful hint embodied in our *Just for Today* leaflet:

Today's Reminder

"Just for today, I will be happy. This assumes to be true what Abraham Lincoln said: 'Most folks are as happy as they make up their minds to be.'

"Nobody's life is *all* dark and cloudy. Let's look for the brighter and happier things in it. This often helps to make the clouds disappear!"

> "Dwelling on our troubles only makes them hurt more. I'll just make myself look on the cheerful side."

"What if. . . ." How often we hear these words from those who live with an alcoholic problem. Only two little words, but they're heavy with dread, fear and anxiety.

"What if he doesn't come home?"—*"What if* she doesn't take care of the children while I'm at work?"—*"What if* he spends all his pay on liquor?"—What if . . . anything our desperate imaginings can project.

Granted these things can happen, but when they don't, we have put ourselves through needless suffering and made ourselves even less prepared to deal with them if they should come.

Today's Reminder

In Al-Anon, the answer to "What if . . ." is "Don't project! Don't imagine the worst; deal with your problems as they arise. Live one day at a time."

I cannot do anything about things that haven't happened; I will not let past experiences make me dread the unknown future.

> "It is a vain and unprofitable thing
> to conceive either grief or joy for
> future things which perhaps will **never**
> come about."

Suppose I decided I want to concentrate on the First Step, shutting out of my mind all other thoughts for just a few minutes. How would I translate it into different words that would impress its meaning on me and guide my attitudes?

"Powerless over alcohol" also says to me: "If I am powerless over it, why do I keep trying to exert my power over another person's drinking?"

It means also: "Let go of your clutching hold on the problem. Let go and let the Divine Power, which works in all things, work in this, too."

If I am powerless over alcohol, my only reasonable course is to Live and Let Live—to learn to live my own life fully and to let others live theirs. Or, more simply, to mind *my own* business.

Today's Reminder

Right now, today, I will lighten my burden by dropping that part of it which does not belong to me. Today I will look more closely at my thoughts and impulses, and take only such action as is required of me.

> "Keep thyself first in peace and then thou wilt be able to bring others to peace. Have, therefore, a zeal in the first place over thyself . . ."
>
> (*Thomas A'Kempis*)

It is not mere chance that brought me to Al-Anon. I was led to it by an unknown power because of my need for the sharing and comfort of others like me. To express my gratitude for this gift I will assume certain responsibilities:

—to study and use the Al-Anon ideas, not only for myself, but for the benefit of my friends in the group.

—to be concerned about their difficulties and to try to help them solve their problems spiritually.

—not to take up the group's time talking about my problems, but to try to make everything I say reflect an Al-Anon teaching which will have meaning for those who hear me.

Today's Reminder

Attending a good Al-Anon meeting is a satisfying experience. Its purpose is far more than just "an evening out". I will prepare myself for these meetings by reading Al-Anon literature so I can pass on something of value. The net result of such full participation will be a better way of life for me.

"We cannot drop out of human involvement without endangering our spiritual health."

Wise words from an AA who counsels with families of alcoholics: "Yes, the alcoholic *can* be forced to get sober."

The spouse: "But I've tried everything. He won't listen to reason. I've yelled and complained, paid the bills, threatened to leave—nothing works."

"Of course not. This is *you* applying the force, and that never works. I suggest you *stop* taking action. The only force that can change the alcoholic's pattern is the pressure that builds up inside him when the family refuses to react any longer. When he can't count on your helping him, when you *won't* assuage his guilt by fighting with him, and you refuse to get him out of trouble—then he'll be compelled to face up to things. In other words, try *inaction* instead of constantly figuring out *something to do* about him."

Today's Reminder

It is not easy to restrain ourselves from reacting to what others do that seems to affect us. A healthy detachment brings about the very changes we were powerless to make by continually fighting the problem.

> "God helps those who don't **try**
> to take over His work."

Complacency is an enemy, easy to recognize in others but difficult to admit in ourselves. It is rarely listed among the major human faults, yet it can hinder us in every form of personal growth.

Complacency simply means being sure we're right, taking it for granted that our view couldn't possibly be wrong. It means judging others by what we think is right. It blocks out understanding and kindness, and justifies qualities in ourselves that we wouldn't find tolerable in other people. Smug complacency is often at the root of family dissension.

Today's Reminder

Let me not be quite so sure that my thinking is always correct. Let me begin by being a little critical of my iron resolution to have things my way. I will keep my ears and my mind open to the ideas of others, even when they don't square with mine. Then I'll be opening the door to growth.

"My serenity does not depend on my winning every round in my battle with life. It does depend on my acceptance of others on their own terms. God grant me that serenity."

Quite frequently we hear a member say that a certain action on the alcoholic's part shows his *immaturity*. This is a favorite label for "what ails him," and according to experts, it is often true.

We come to Al-Anon, however, not to take inventory of others, but of ourselves. It is because we, too, are immature individuals that we are attracted to alcoholics as marriage partners—a sort of child-calling-to-child.

If immaturity is giving me trouble, I will examine my own reactions, and work on them.

Wrangling with the alcoholic over petty matters is immature. So are sulking and tears and devious tricks to outwit him. So are many other things *some of us* do, at least some of the time.

Today's Reminder

The task is clearly set before me: to fix what's out of kilter with me; to check my temptation to play childish games in a deadly serious human dilemma. Correcting my own shortcomings will improve matters for everyone concerned.

"Maturity is the capacity to withstand ego-destroying experiences, and not lose one's perspective in the ego-building experiences."

(*Robert K. Greenleaf*)

Few of us are entirely free from a sense of guilt. We may be remorseful because of our words or actions, or for things left undone. We may even feel guilty because of irrational or false accusations by the alcoholic.

When I am troubled by a feeling of guilt, I cannot put into my day all I am capable of. I must rid myself of this feeling, not by pushing it aside, but by identifying it and correcting the cause.

Free of this weight, I can put all of my best into my day's work and my spiritual growth. Then I will have something worthwhile to give others, instead of concentrating on my own frustrations.

Today's Reminder

I will refuse to be troubled by an uneasy sense of guilt. I will track it to its source and make good for any harm I have done. I will be most careful not to whitewash it with self-justification and self-righteousness. That would hamper everything I am trying to accomplish.

> "A man is relieved and gay when he has
> put his heart into his work and done his
> best; but what he has said or done other-
> wise shall give him no peace."
(Ralph Waldo Emerson: *Essay on Self-Reliance*)

A phrase that turns up quite often in Al-Anon meetings is: "Yes, but . . ."

Member A is explaining how an Al-Anon idea can be applied to B's problem. B, interrupting, says: "Yes, but . . ." and proceeds to show how different her case is, and how much worse than others, and that it couldn't possibly be solved by anything as simple as applying a Step or a Slogan, for example.

"Yes, but . . ." means she's not ready to listen because she doesn't want her problem under-rated. She's been living with it, and only she knows how awful it is. She overlooks the fact that we're all there for the same reasons.

Today's Reminder

If ever I am tempted to say "Yes, but . . ." I will remind myself to concentrate on what my Al-Anon friend is saying. If I'm sure I want to make my life more livable, I'll listen with an open mind, and apply what I hear.

The key to Al-Anon is *to accept and use the program* without any of the "Yes, buts" that would reveal only my resistance and uncertainty.

> "I will not resist the impact of a new idea.
> It may be just the one I've needed
> without being aware of it. I will make
> my mind more flexible and receptive
> to new points of view."

As members of an Al-Anon group, we attend meetings, keep in touch with the others, read, meditate and pray. It's wonderful to realize that this participation also makes us part of a world-wide network of groups, all working for the same purpose: to build better lives for ourselves and those around us. Imagine the immense power for good that is generated by such a fellowship as ours.

Al-Anon members on every continent, in such faraway places as Australia, Japan, Finland, Uruguay and the South Sea Islands—all are my brothers and sisters. What I do is helping them; what they do helps me.

Nationality, race, color, religion, wealth, poverty—all these do not matter to us as members of this great loving fellowship.

Today's Reminder

As I talk with my hometown friends in Al-Anon, I realize that we are all part of something much bigger than our single group. I will remember, and send loving thoughts to those in our thousands of groups around the world. This exchange will enrich all of us.

> "This is truly a movement of the spirit,
> and I firmly believe that the unity of
> the world, in understanding and peace,
> could come from these efforts . . ."
> *(a member in New Zealand)*

Wanting to know why the alcoholic drinks or, when sober, why he does what he does, is "an itch for which there is no scratch."

Some of us never get over trying to figure it out. Since we're not psychiatrists, our researches are bound to end in frustration, so let's accept it as impossible—and also unimportant.

What *is* important, and within our God-given powers to figure out, is what *we* are doing that confuses and complicates life for us. When we discover that, and do something to change it, a good many of our troubles will vanish.

Today's Reminder

Every time I catch myself trying to figure out other people's motives, I'll stop and ask myself: "What did I say or do that prompted the action? Why did I react to it as I did? Does what happened make a major difference to me, or am I making something big out of a trifle?"

"Leave off that excessive desire of
   knowing; therein is found much distraction.
   There are many things the knowledge of
   which is of little or no profit to the
   soul."

(*Thomas A'Kempis*)

I can take strength and comfort from knowing I belong to the Al-Anon fellowship, with its world-wide membership all working together for the same purpose. Our little group is but one of thousands.

What holds us together, our many different nationalities and faiths? There are no rules and regulations, no management control, nobody to say "you must do this" or "you may not do that." There is, however, government by principle, as stated in the Twelve Traditions, which each member, and each group accepts.

Each of us in his own way works for the good of the others. What binds us together is a common problem to be solved by understanding and mutual service. Al-Anon runs—like the little wheel in the old song—by the grace of God.

Today's Reminder

I belong to Al-Anon. It is an important part of my life because it unites me, in thought and action, to people all over the world who share my desire to fill life with meaning and purpose. I do not know them, but they are my friends, and I am theirs. The more each of us lives by Al-Anon's spiritual principles, the more we help each other, no matter how great a distance may separate us.

> "I thank God for helping me to find
> Al-Anon which is showing me the way
> to a new life."

An Al-Anon member may devote a lot of
time to reading scientific books on alcoholism,
because she imagines it will make her better
able to cope with "the problem." Unless we
intend to become professionals in the field,
nothing is to be gained by an in-depth study of
the disease.

Nor does it help to explore the reasons for
the alcoholic's behavior; certainly not while
our own conduct shows we are not entirely
rational. So, again, all change must begin with
us.

The search should be for *our own* serenity;
which will prove to have remarkable power to
inspire others in the home.

Today's Reminder

Do I read up on alcoholism because I still hope
I can find a way to make my spouse stop drinking?
Do I blame all the family's adversities on the
alcoholic, sober or not? Have I the courage to face
my own mistakes and character flaws? Do I justify
my resentment and rationalize my self-pity?

> "How much trouble he avoids who does not
> look to see what others say or do, but
> only what he does himself, that it may
> be just and pure."
>   (Marcus Aurelius: *Meditations*)

When my spirit is in turmoil and my troubled thoughts race round and round, and I try to *reason myself* out of this frame of mind, it may be well to *stop reasoning* and hold fast to a single idea that speaks of quiet and serenity. One such is: *Keep It Simple.*

Probably there is nothing I can do now—this minute, this hour, today—to solve the problem that is gnawing at my peace of mind. Then to what purpose do I torment myself?

I will stop trying to figure out ways and means. I will not rehash, over and over, thoughts so bitter that they can make me feel physically ill. I will empty my mind of all this perplexity and hold to just one simple thought while I wait for God's guidance.

Today's Reminder

The things that trouble me are often too complex to yield to human reasoning. Indeed their only reality may be in my confused thoughts. When I reach such an impasse and I remind myself to *keep it simple,* I will find myself being restored to composure.

"Under the shadow of Thy wing shall be
my refuge until this tyranny be overpast."
(*Book of Common Prayer*)

The newcomer to Al-Anon usually feels alone in a hostile world, drowning in a sea of troubles. To be sure, some may have been of her own making, but all of us had much to learn about living with an alcoholic before we could begin to create a serene and orderly world within us.

Let us not be too eager to swamp this confused person with advice. A warm welcome and words of hope and reassurance will be all the therapy she can use at first. One member, too, should offer a protecting wing and a willing ear to her troubles, if she cares to talk about them after the meeting.

Today's Reminder

Each of us should take thought for the newcomer. Her coming to Al-Anon can enrich our lives, as well as helping her. She brings us an opportunity to introduce her to the healing help of the Al-Anon program. We profit by such giving; as we share with her what we have learned, our own thoughts are clarified by new insights. It also helps us to realize how much insight we have gained since we were beginners in the fellowship.

> "I pray to be guided in my efforts to
> help a newcomer. Let me be selective
> in my sharing of experience, strength
> and hope, to make sure his or her needs
> are met."

We hear and read, over and over again, that we are powerless over alcohol, and that the alcoholic's sobriety is not our business or our responsibility. It may seem paradoxical, then, to assert that we, the spouses, can have a tremendous influence in bringing about sobriety and helping the alcoholic to maintain it.

When we continue to nag and domineer, complain and criticize, we are assuming, in large measure, the responsibility for *deferred* sobriety, and for slips *from* sobriety.

Al-Anon shows us how to change these destructive attitudes. As we abandon the role of accuser, judge and manager, the home climate shows marked improvement. A pleasant, cheerful environment, which we can create, often creates in the alcoholic a desire to get sober.

Today's Reminder

Being powerless over alcohol and the alcoholic simply means that it cannot be done by forcing issues. A change in our attitude, on the other hand, has limitless power to bring serenity and order into the home.

> "I am not powerless over myself,
> and the way I act and react. This
> is, in itself, a power that can work
> miracles in changing the attitudes of
> others."

The simplest—and most difficult—of all our slogans is the word THINK. We seem to be thinking hard all the time, but it is mostly about our troubles, and who's to blame for them. We can't seem to get around to thinking about what *we* may be doing that damages us. One word to think about is *retaliation*.

Have I ever thought, in some form or other: "I'll fix him for that!" "I'll pay her back for what she did." Do I seek relief from my resentment by retaliation, instead of forgiveness?

If a person hurts me without being aware of it, and I can overlook it, my reward is an inner glow. If the alcohol-heated spouse expresses his self-hatred in strong language directed at me, I know it has no validity and so I can ignore it.

Today's Reminder

Before I take any action—or speak any hot words—I will think about what provoked me into this impulse. If I can persuade myself not to act or speak, I can quietly and inwardly rejoice that my Higher Power gave me the grace to be silent.

Such constructive thinking is a fine ego-builder —just one of many.

> "What shall it profit a man to be
> right if he thereby make an enemy?"

What if there were no such problem as alcoholism in the world? Would all marriages, and all other human relationships, be therefore perfect? Of course not! Then it should be easy to realize that sobriety cannot bring release from all our problems.

True, alcoholism can wreck marriages that might otherwise have had a good chance of success. But it is also true that the basic adjustments to each other must somehow be made.

Al-Anon's prime purpose is to help us deal with the problems that alcoholism has *aggravated*. But just as important is its usefulness in helping us to adjust to our partners—and to other people.

Today's Reminder

If I really want to learn how to fit easily and happily into my environment and my relations with other people, Al-Anon has something for me. Once I have met the problem of alcoholism which introduced me to the program, I expect to go on using it for the rest of my life.

> "We all of us need some kind of a philosophy to live by," commented an AA speaker, "so I'll just settle for the Twelve Steps."

One thing about Al-Anon that hardly anyone ever mentions—or even realizes—is that it makes life so much easier for us. When we're told the advantages of studying the Twelve Steps, reading the literature, attending meetings, we may think: "They're always giving me something to do!" But all the things suggested in Al-Anon are for *our* benefit—precisely to make life more pleasant and livable. Are we trapped in problems? Al-Anon points the way to solutions. Our fellow members even lead us by the hand and show us how they applied to themselves the wonderful, *relieving* ideas we're learning.

Today's Reminder

The effects of the Al-Anon program are revealed to me as a series of little miracles, as each day lifts another burden because I am changing my way of thinking about it.

I will follow this program as though my life depended on it, as indeed it does, if by life I mean real living—joyous and comfortable.

> "To resist spiritual guidance is to defeat ourselves. The Al-Anon program is a spiritual way of life."

I will begin today to include an Al-Anon Quiet Time in each day, remembering this especially in times of family upheavals and dissension. If *I* provide the element of quiet in my home, I will at least not be adding to the turmoil.

Quiet can be achieved with complete silence, but if the silence has in it even a trace of anger or hostility, it loses all its power. A grim silence is even more challenging to a combatant than speech. True quiet has the quality of serenity, acceptance, peace.

I must remind myself of this constantly in times of stress.

Today's Reminder

I can persuade myself to be quiet by realizing that angry words cannot touch me unless I allow them to. Most angry words have no basis in logic or reason anyway, so why need they hurt me? If a wrathful explosion on the alcoholic's part seems aimed at me, I will understand that it may only express his own guilt; I will not allow this to be shifted to my shoulders.

> "In quiet and in silence the truth
> is made clear. . . ."

How many waking hours are there in this day? What will I do with them? Today, this day, is all the time I have to do anything with, so I will use it with care. I will not waste a moment of it worrying about yesterdays; nor will I let a thought of dread for tomorrow cross my mind.

I will use this time for my essential duties, perhaps tackling the hard ones first so I won't be tempted to "put off until tomorrow." I will plan some little time for enjoyment and relaxation, and some, even if only ten minutes, for solitary meditation and prayer.

Today's Reminder

This day belongs to me. I can do wonderful things with it, creative things, including the creation of order in my surroundings and in my mind. Nobody else owns my particular segment of time, so it depends only on me how well I will fill every moment to my satisfaction.

Al-Anon tells me to live one day at a time. This is that day.

> "Just for today I will be unafraid.
> Especially I will not be afraid to
> enjoy what is beautiful and to believe
> that as I give to the world, so the
> world will give to me."
> 　　　　(from Al-Anon's "Just for Today.")

I would like to look back over this month and see what progress I have made, and what changes have taken place in my life as a result of my practicing the Al-Anon program.

Have I given sufficient attention to the Twelve Steps? Have I done at least a little reading each day? Are my family relationships more serene and happy than they were a month ago? Have I renewed a strained friendship; made good for an injury to someone, made an effort to avoid gossip, tried to learn something new?

Today's Reminder

This will be my day of review and preparation for the coming month in which I will renew my efforts to progress in my personal development.

If I cannot see any improvement in the month which is ending today, I will not be discouraged for, among other things, I must learn to accept myself as I am. Everything good I can bring about must begin with that.

> "An occasional review of my progress is an encouraging exercise, for it shows me that I am gradually learning how to live in poise and serenity."

Perhaps many of us have had the thought, at one time and another, "Oh, if I could only run away from all this and start all over again."

We think a fresh beginning would solve everything; that we wouldn't make the same mistakes again, and so we'd have a chance to be happy.

Of course we know this is a childish fantasy. The very idea that we can entertain such a notion should make us a little doubtful of our maturity. For we know perfectly well— admit it or not—that we'd be taking our troubles with us. We can't run away from ourselves.

Isn't this clear proof that many of our troubles are self-created—many of our personal agonies self-inflicted?

Today's Reminder

A big step toward maturing is to realize that I cannot change conditions by running away from them. I can only change my point of view about them and their relation to me—and this can be done only by changing myself.

"Little by little I can change my world— not by escaping to a new one with the same old me, but by making a *new me* out of the old one."

The Al-Anon slogans are little pieces of advice. If we were entirely capable of putting them all into practice, we'd be pretty close to perfection as spiritual human beings.

Take this one, for instance: *Live and let live.* A whole philosophy of life is condensed into these four words. First we are admonished to live—to live fully, richly, happily, and to fulfill our destiny with the joy that comes from doing well whatever we do. Then comes a more difficult admonition: *Let live.* This means acknowledging the right of every other human being to live as he wants to, without criticism or judgment from us. It rules out contempt for those who do not think as we do. It warns against resentment; tells us to avoid construing other people's actions as intentional injuries to us.

Today's Reminder

The more I think about living, and letting others live, the more I will learn from it. I will try to make it my yardstick in everything I do, and especially in relating to the people in my life.

"When my thoughts are centered on learning
to live, I will be less tempted to involve
my mind with the thoughts of how others live."

Sometimes I find myself so busy wondering what someone else is doing, and where and why, that my own thoughts create turmoil inside me. When this happens, I know I'm a candidate for a new, honest, self-appraisal. If I allow myself to evade this self-confrontation, I'll be a candidate for a rude awakening!

I must not forget that my first obligation is to work out changes in my own thinking patterns. My progress toward becoming a worthwhile human being depends on making these changes, and so does the improvement I long for in the circumstances of my life.

Today's Reminder

I can change nothing but myself. Do I need changing? If things are going wrong—or seem to be—maybe it's because of the way *I'm* reacting to them. If I accept the fact that the principal source of my unhappiness is in me, I'll be giving myself a good reason to do something about *me*. It isn't easy—but the rewards are beyond reckoning!

> "My happiness cannot possibly depend
> on my forcing changes in somebody else.
> Nor does my misery come from anyone but
> myself."

One source of frustration we seldom recognize is in *expecting* too much of others, or *expecting* too specifically what we feel they ought to be, say, give or do.

If I *expect* another person to react in a certain way to a given situation, and he or she fails to meet my expectation, have I the right to be disappointed or angry?

Every human being has his own individual drives and motivations, beyond my understanding and control. I may say: "But he *knew* what I *expected*," not realizing that it may have been precisely for this reason that he rebelled and acted otherwise.

My search for peace of mind will bear fruit much more readily if I stop *expecting* and relax into acceptance.

Today's Reminder

I will not set a pattern based on my own experience and wishes—and expect someone else to live up to it. This is interference of a subtle and damaging kind; it damages my peace of mind and dignity, and those I am smothering with my expectations.

> "I, too, often fail to live up to
> the expectations of others."

What we get from our association with Al-Anon depends pretty much on what we put into it. Certainly the Al-Anon program can help me rid myself of my despairs and frustrations, but the major effort of listening, observing and concentrating must be mine. Al-Anon points the way, but we must take the road. Al-Anon provides the tools, but we must use them.

Today's Reminder

If I apply myself to the Al-Anon program, do some reading from an Al-Anon book every day, regard my meetings as too important to be missed, and I apply what I am learning, I'm on the road. Along the way I can help others to work out their problems, and so gain further help from my willingness to share what I am getting from Al-Anon.

I want to be constantly aware of my role as a member of this fellowship, consciously experience the comforting interchange this membership makes possible. It is as though I had found a secure island, inhabited by loving and interested friends.

> "The reason I make so much of being
> an Al-Anon member is that Al-Anon
> has been the means of making a better
> person of me."

This is a day which God has given into my hands. If I could only realize what a tremendous gift this is, I would use every moment of it to make my life more serene, more rewarding. I would not look back over my shoulder at the disappointments of the past—I would not anxiously contemplate the future. I would live—just for today—as well as I can. I would put aside critical thoughts of others. I would notice interesting things—the expressions on people's faces, a plant growing on my windowsill, the grace and charm of a child, an arrangement of clouds. Today there are wonders all around me, if I will open my eyes and enjoy them.

Today's Reminder

Let me not be so preoccupied with thoughts of my grievances and troubles that today's good can escape me. Today I can begin a new way of using my minutes and hours, a new way of looking at my surroundings and the circumstances of my life. I will make this day one I can look back upon with pleasure and satisfaction and a preparation for the days to come.

> "Today is all the time I have. Nobody can keep me from using it well. If I make this a good day, tomorrow can be even better."

"Use a slogan," somebody suggests at a meeting. "Keep it in the forefront of your mind all the time, and don't let your troubles crowd it out. Act on it!"

Take, for example, *"Let Go and Let God."*

The more tightly I clutch my problems to my mind, the less opportunity I give God to help me work them out. The more tensely and desperately I try to solve them, the more the answers elude me.

I will let go and let God. If I can't solve my difficulty, perhaps He will, if I can only let go and let Him.

Today's Reminder

Saying this small phrase over and over gives me such a sense of release and relaxation that nothing seems as difficult as before. The thought of just letting go seems to drop a heavy weight from my shoulders, and lets me breathe freely again. Why has it been so hard for me to let go? Is it because I feel that only I am capable of solving the big problems? I know that isn't true, so I will just Let Go and Let God.

> God's help is always available; all
> we have to do is to make room for Him
> to take part in our lives and keep
> ourselves ready to accept His guidance

We hear it said that Al-Anon members do not give each other advice. This refers specifically to the kind of advice that suggests taking drastic action to bring about a radical change in a marriage relationship. This we do not—and must not—do.

In other ways, we in Al-Anon give a great deal of advice. We suggest looking into ourselves for the causes of our problems; we advise dependence on God's guidance. We recommend lots of Al-Anon reading, the study of the Twelve Steps and the Slogans. We suggest spiritual ways to find a new perspective and new strength, and share our personal experience in applying them.

Today's Reminder

When I am greatly troubled by an insoluble problem, I will gladly accept the advice of my fellow members that I concentrate on a Slogan or a Step in finding a solution. I know that constructive action can be taken only after I have lifted my thoughts and emotions out of their confused state.

> Using the Slogans and the Twelve Steps will strengthen me to make wise decisions.

I know how easy it is to let anger well up inside me at the thought of someone who has injured me. What is much more difficult is to take a detached view so we can stop the building up of this "head of steam." Unless I do this, it will explode, damaging me and everything around me.

When we are frustrated in our desire to punish the one we're angry at, we may take it out on innocent bystanders, sometimes even our own children, those young lives which God has entrusted to our hands. Surely we have an obligation—a duty of love—to avoid aggravating the emotional damage that the drinking parent may already be inflicting on them.

Today's Reminder

There are many good reasons to keep myself from harboring resentful thoughts. They can grow into savage attacks on other human beings. Another good reason for quieting my anger before it gets out of hand is to prevent the emotional scars it can leave on me.

> "If any man among you seem to be
> religious and bridleth not his tongue,
> he deceiveth his own heart; this man's
> religion is vain."
>
> (*General Epistle of James*)

In the book of Proverbs we read: "The stroke of the tongue breaketh the bones. Weigh thy words in a balance and make a door and a bar for thy mouth. Envy and wrath shorten the life."

This statement speaks directly for the Al-Anon program. We are constantly being reminded that we are working to improve ourselves, to protect ourselves from the influences of confusion, anger and resentment.

In these words from the Bible we have a direct recommendation to check our part in the difficulties we have with others. And the reason it gives—*our own benefit*—is equally valid in Al-Anon teachings.

Today's Reminder

Let me reflect how much damage I may have done, and may still do, by saying the first thing that comes to mind. Let me realize that the worst reaction of unbridled anger falls upon me. What I say in a single moment of uncontrolled rage can have inconceivable long-range consequences.

> "Be swift to hear, slow to speak,
>   slow to wrath, for the wrath of man
>   worketh not the righteousness of God."
>   (*General Epistle of James*)

Even with a growing understanding of Al-Anon philosophy, we might find it difficult to accept such a statement as this:

"Al-Anon is a way to personal freedom."

Suppose I feel like a prisoner, trapped in an irksome way of life, as so many of us do. What am I doing about it? My obvious impulse is to try to manipulate the things and people around me into being more acceptable to me. Do I argue, rage and weep to make my spouse behave in a way that I think will make me happier? Happiness isn't won that way.

Freedom from despair and frustration can come only from changing, *in myself*, the attitudes that are maintaining the conditions that cause me grief.

Today's Reminder

I have the power to set myself free by conquering the personal shortcomings that chain me to my problems. And not the least of these is the short-sightedness that has made me refuse to accept responsibility for the way I am.

> "Be not overcome of evil, but overcome
> evil with good."
>
> (*Romans*)

It is difficult to overcome the habit of setting standards for our spouses, and expecting them to be followed. Unfortunately this may continue even after the alcoholic is sober in AA. We figure out what the results of his sobriety should be, in changed attitudes and behavior and, when things don't work out the way we expect, we're frustrated and angry.

I must teach myself to leave my partner to God and to his friends in AA. I must learn not to expect or demand. I will look for, and appreciate, his positive and desirable actions, and not concentrate on the negative. I must, in other words, do something constructive about my own attitude.

Today's Reminder

I will not look for perfection in another person until I have attained perfection myself. Since I know this will never be, let me learn to accept things as they are, and stop manipulating them into changing. Let me look for a wiser approach to life *from myself*, not from other people.

> "Thou must learn to renounce thy
> own will in many things, if thou
> wilt keep peace and concord with
> others."
>
> (*Thomas A'Kempis*)

We suffer more than we need to, and often, perhaps, because we want to. Many of us reopen old wounds by dwelling on the past— what "he or she did last week or last year." Many of us live in needless dread of what tomorrow will bring.

An interesting and rewarding exercise for today might be to examine all the things that are hurting me at the moment. I will challenge their validity to see if there is any basis for my bitterness—or for that dread and fear. I'll probably discover, to my delight, that I have, right at this moment, more than enough reasons to be happy and contented.

Today's Reminder

Why do I allow myself to suffer? Is there any meaning or validity to the items I am permitting myself to suffer from? What if "he said this"— or "she did that". Even if it was *meant* to hurt, it cannot reach the real me, if I stand guard at the door of my mind.

> "Some of your hurts you have cured,
>   And the sharpest you've even survived,
>   But what torments of grief you've endured,
>   From evils which never arrived."
>   (*Ralph Waldo Emerson*)

When an alcoholic finally reaches bottom,
and begins the long climb upward through AA,
this is the beginning of growth in personal and
spiritual maturity.

If we grant, as surely we must, that both
partners in an alcoholic marriage are or have
become neurotic, we non-alcoholics, too, need
the help of a growth program.

If A, then, takes steps to get well and face
life as a responsible adult, how can B keep
pace without the self-understanding that eventually comes to us in Al-Anon? This is the
practical logic of the words of our Suggested
Welcome: "Working in unity for a common
purpose does more than strengthen both partners individually. It draws them together."

Today's Reminder

If the AA member recognizes that sobriety is
only the beginning of his growth, the spouse, too,
needs continuing help in adjusting to the new
problems of their joint relationship. Al-Anon shows
us how to meet that responsibility with dignity
grace and love.

> ". . . that our loves and comforts
> should increase even as our days
> do grow."

Each of us has, as a person, an enormous potential. Many of our frustrations come from not making the most of ourselves and getting out of life what it has to give, ready and waiting for us to accept.

Although we come into Al-Anon to deal with a specific problem, we do not always realize that developing ourselves could be the answer, not only to the problem of living with alcoholism, but to others as well.

The solutions rest with me. With the help of my Higher Power, I can adorn my life with comfort, serenity and enjoyment. It does not depend on any other person, and the sooner I accept this fact, the sooner I will be able to face myself realistically.

Today's Reminder

People can affect me only as I allow them to. I need not be influenced by others, for I am free to consult my own wishes and standards, and decide what is best for me. I find I can realize my own strength and confidence by working faithfully with the Al-Anon program, and using it in my daily life.

> ". . . the only real answer to frustration is to concern myself with the drawing forth of what is uniquely me. This gives me the impulse and the courage to act constructively on the outside world."
>
> (*Robert K. Greenleaf*)

It may be that the harsh words and accusations we use to whip the alcoholic for what he has done, or failed to do, leave no mark once the battle is over. But how can we tell? How can we risk hurting another person who is already so deeply wounded by his own guilt?

Does the voice of God have a chance to be heard over my angry shouting? What is the purpose of letting myself fly apart in reckless tantrums? To punish the drinker? To relieve my pent-up feelings?

Today's Reminder

I cannot punish anyone without punishing myself. The release of my tensions, even if it seems justified, leaves dregs of bitterness behind. Unless I have deliberately decided that my relationship with my spouse has no further value in my life, I would do well to consider the long-range benefits of quiet acceptance in times of stress.

> "How shall you punish those whose
> remorse is already greater than
> their misdeeds?"
> (Kahlil Gibran, *The Prophet*)

We sometimes forget what a painful experience it was to come to our first Al-Anon meeting. Remember the whirling thoughts, the fears, the uncertainty? Uneasy questions came crowding into our minds: "Is it the right thing to do?"—"What will *he* say if he finds out?"—"Am I disgracing my family by admitting that husband and father drinks too much?"—"What if somebody tells I was there?"

Then we were reassured to discover that Al-Anon has a protective cloak of anonymity for us. Every member understands that no word of the proceedings must ever go beyond the meeting room, and especially that no names should ever be mentioned.

Today's Reminder

The newcomer to Al-Anon immediately feels comforted and safe when she learns that she can talk freely without fear of having anything repeated. We owe her this assurance. We are committed to it by our own Traditions, as well as by our personal need for protection against careless gossip.

I will remind myself daily that I must guard against revealing anything concerning Al-Anon or an AA member.

> Tradition Twelve: Anonymity is the
> spiritual foundation of all our
> Traditions, ever reminding us to
> place principles above personalities.

Some of us had a long list of grievances against the alcoholic, especially while the drinking was still active. The worst possible thing we can do is to remember them, dwell on them, and polish up our halos of martyrdom. The very best we can do is to erase them from memory, so each new day becomes an opportunity to make things better.

It is not my assignment to keep an inventory of my spouse's faults and misbehaviors. My task is to watch for my own and root them out, so that what I say and do will help to make things better for me and for my family.

Today's Reminder

Storing up grievances is more than a waste of time; it's a waste of life that could be lived to greater satisfaction. If I keep a record of oppressions and indignities, I am restoring them to painful reality.

I've found they're surprisingly easy to forget, once I start using the Al-Anon program each day.

"The horror of that moment," the King said,
"I shall never, never forget."
"You will, though," said the Queen, "if you
don't make a memorandum of it."
(Lewis Carroll: *Through the Looking Glass*)

My attitude toward another—whether drinking or not—can have untold influence on the life of my family. Perhaps, through long drinking years, I acquired the habit of tearing him down, showing my contempt for his actions, indignation at the neglect of obligations. I am responsible for the consequences of such attitudes. Even a little understanding and compassion will show us that our behavior is ego-destroying, and the ego of the drinker is already painfully battered by guilt and fear.

Today's Reminder

I never want to forget that my spouse, with whatever faults he or she may have, is a child of God, and is therefore entitled to my respect and consideration. I will guard against assuming the role of judge and punisher, for I cannot destroy another person without inflicting great damage on myself.

> "It is easy, terribly easy, to
>   shake a man's faith in himself.
> To take advantage of that to
>   break a man's spirit, is devil's
>   work."
>
> (G. B. Shaw: *Candida*)

A member whose husband had recently joined AA was recounting her current experiences: "He doesn't go to enough meetings to keep him sober. I noticed that the level of the Scotch was a little below the mark I had made on the bottle. He doesn't want me to go to AA meetings with him, but I go anyway; I have to see how this AA works."

Another member answers: "You're treating him like a baby in a play-pen—watching him perform—deciding what he ought to be doing. Who put you in charge of your husband? Why do you think you know what's right for him? Accept the fact that he's trying, and let him find his sobriety in his own way."

Today's Reminder

It's sometimes a shock to have our thinking errors pointed out to us, but I must always remember that in Al-Anon the motive is loving and helpful.

If I'm on the wrong track, I want to know it so I can correct my faulty attitude. Others can often see our problems more clearly than we can, and from that we get our best help.

> "Teach me to think straight, and not
> to take offense at criticism which is
> meant as loving guidance."

If I believe that it is hopeless to expect any improvement in my life, I am doubting the power of God. If I believe I have reason for despair, I am confessing personal failure, for I *do* have the power to change myself, and nothing can prevent it but my own unwillingness.

Never let me imagine that my satisfaction with life depends on what someone else may do. This is a thinking error I can get rid of in Al-Anon. I can learn to avail myself of the immense, inexhaustible power of God, if I am willing to be *continually* conscious of God's nearness.

Today's Reminder

I am not at the mercy of a cruel or capricious fate, for I have the power to determine what my life will be. I am not alone. I have the confidence and faith of all Al-Anon to support my efforts, as it is expressed by the loving concern and help of the friends in my group. I am not alone, because God is with me whenever I make myself aware of Him.

> "To be without hope is to deny the wonderful possibilities of the future."

If a sharp thorn or a splinter pierces my hand, what do I do? I remove it as quickly as I can. Surely I wouldn't leave it there, hurting me, until it festered and sent its infection throughout my body.

Yet what do I do with the thorns of resentment and hatred when *they* pierce my thoughts? Do I leave them there and watch them grow, while I suffer increasingly from the pain?

True, resentment and hatred are more difficult to pull out of our thoughts than the physical thorn from a finger, but so much depends upon it that I will do my best to eliminate them, before their poison can spread.

Today's Reminder

If I really do not want to be hurt, and if I am sure that self-pity isn't giving me a certain secret satisfaction, I will take all the steps necessary to free my mind from painful thoughts and emotions. The best way to do this is not by grimly exerting will power, but by replacing those hurting ideas with thoughts of love and gratitude.

> "Thou has not half the power to do me
> harm, as I have to be hurt."
>   (William Shakespeare: *Othello*)

We learn so much in Al-Anon, and in such interesting and unexpected ways. In the midst of a somewhat bantering interchange at a meeting, everyone suddenly laughed at something that was said. "Wait a minute," one member interrupted. "Everyone around this table is smiling—we've all put aside our griefs and our grievances. Do we behave in this cheerful way at home, or do we automatically put on our *martyr-face*? I know I do—and right now I'm going to begin to change that."

Today's Reminder

Do I habitually wear my martyr-face to remind my spouse what a hard time he's giving me? Or do I try to lift his spirits—already so depressed by guilt and confusion? Will I try—really try— from now on, to be pleasant and a bit gay, even when things aren't going my way? Am I afraid to let those around me know I do have some reasons to be happy, or do I want everybody to feel sorry for me?

". . . that thou art happy, thou owest to God; that thou continuest such, thou owest to thyself."

(John Milton: *Paradise Lost*)

Somewhere along the line, in our study of the Al-Anon program, we reach a sharp realization of the growth-value of honesty and candor. When this happens, one of the first things we are able to admit is that our behavior, like that of the alcoholic, has been far from sane and reasonable. When we can do this, without shame or embarrassment, we seem to break free of a hampering shell.

This is progress, but let's not imagine that Al-Anon has done all it can for us. We have reached a plateau; there are still more heights to climb, to reach serenity and a full life.

Today's Reminder

If ever I come to the complacent conclusion that I don't need Al-Anon any longer, let me remind myself that it can do far more than to carry me through the anguish of living with the problems of alcoholism.

I know I can make even greater strides in fulfilling myself, for Al-Anon is a philosophy, a way of life; I will never outgrow the need for it.

> "Once I have overcome the problems
> that first brought me into this
> fellowship, I am confident that my
> continuing search for spiritual
> understanding will yield ever richer
> benefits."

Have I ever accomplished anything good while my emotions were churning with hysteria? Am I aware that reacting on impulse— saying the first thing that pops into my head— defeats my own purposes? I couldn't lose by stopping to think: *Easy does it*. Wouldn't any crisis shrink to manageable size if I could wait a little while to figure out what is best to do? Unless I'm sure I'm pouring oil on troubled waters, and not on a raging fire, it might be best to do and say nothing until things calm down. Easy does it.

Today's Reminder

It may take a bit of self-control to back away from conflict and confusion. But it's wonderful protection for my peace of mind. Unless I can say or do something to quell the storm, I'll only be inflicting punishment on myself. And each little battle I win—*with myself*—makes the next one easier. Take it easy, for easy does it. It will all seem much less important tomorrow!

> "Quietness is a great ally, my friend.
> As long as I keep my poise, I will
> do nothing to make bad matters worse."

Someone at an Al-Anon meeting said: "My wife has been around AA for ten years, and has never made a first anniversary. She almost completes the year, and then something happens that sets her off to drinking again. It may not last more than a few days, but these repeated lapses are so frustrating that I wonder if she'll ever make it."

This is a problem Al-Anon is well able to solve. It was pointed out to him that the long periods of sobriety were cause for rejoicing; that he should appreciate the earnest effort his spouse made to stay sober, and not condemn her lapses. And above all, that the problem is not his, but hers, and does not have to affect his life as an individual.

Today's Reminder

Too often I take the alcoholic's struggles unto myself and feel that I should be able to do something about them. When I find myself slipping into this God-like attitude, I'll do a little concentrating on the First Step—"admitted we were powerless. . . ."

> "Why art thou troubled because things do not succeed with thee according to thy desire? Who is there who hath all things according to his will? Neither I, nor thou, nor any man upon earth."
>
> (*Thomas A'Kempis*)

An interesting exercise, and one well worth a few moments of reflection, would be to consider the exact meaning of the phrase *"to take offense."*

These words describe an act of willingly taking into ourselves a hurt we feel somebody intended to inflict on us. We *take* offense. We don't have to take it. We are free to refuse to be hurt by a spiteful remark or malicious action.

So the whole matter really rests with us. The choice of accepting or rejecting an offense is ours alone.

Today's Reminder

It may not be easy at first, but if I keep reminding myself that I will not permit myself to be hurt by what anyone says or does, it can bring about an amazing change in my attitude and disposition.

Whenever I feel I am being hurt by someone, I will silently refuse to *take* offense, or take any action to retaliate. What a relief it will be to have such incidents vanish into thin air, leaving not a mark on me! I will not *accept* offense.

> "What can words do to me unless
> I take them to heart?"

There is one meaning to the phrase "forgetting myself" that admonishes me not to lose my temper. When someone says something rash or ugly, we say they are "forgetting themselves," meaning they are forgetting their *best* selves in a sudden fit of uncontrolled anger.

Someone at an Al-Anon meeting spoke of this in telling how her mother helped her overcome a fiery temper when she was a little girl:

"Whenever I had a tantrum, my mother would say very quietly: 'You're forgetting yourself, dear; mod-u-late your voice and then it won't hurt so much.' That always brought me up short and made me ashamed. Once I answered, All right, mother, I will *remember* myself, and finally all she had to say was: 'Forgetting yourself? Modulate . . .' and we'd both laugh."

Today's Reminder

If I remember the kind of person I want to be, I won't forget myself and yield to an angry surge of temper. I will remember to modulate my voice —quiet always sets the stage for calm.

"Forget not thyself in times of anger. . ."

How many of my frustrations and disappointments come from expecting too much! It is good to set our standards high, but only if we are prepared to accept, with unperturbed serenity, results that fall short of what we expect.

We expect more of the alcoholic than a sick, confused human can deliver. Once he is sober, we expect a complete transformation. Above all, we make too great demands on ourselves.

Today's Reminder

Let me learn to settle for less than I *wish* were possible, and be willing to accept it and appreciate it. I will not expect too much of anyone, not even of myself. Contentment comes from accepting gratefully the good that comes to us, and not from raging at life because it is not better. This wholesome attitude is by no means *resignation*, but a realistic acceptance.

"What you have may seem small; you desire so
  much more. See children thrusting their hands
  into a narrow-necked jar, striving to pull out
  the sweets. If they fill the hand, they cannot pull it out and then they fall to tears.
  When they let go a few, they can draw out the
  rest. You, too, let your desire go; covet not
  too much. . ."

                                    (*Epictetus*)

When a family situation becomes really desperate, and we think we just can't go on another day living in uncertainty, fear, deprivation and general misery, we may decide to take action. That's good. But what action? So much depends on taking the right course. Let me consider:

Is my present frame of mind, whether of anger, bitterness or confusion, one in which I can make a wise choice? Have I yielded too readily to friendly advice, well-meant, but based on only limited knowledge of all the factors?

Today's Reminder

If I have come to the end of my rope, I have lived in this turmoil for a long time. Let me be patient a little longer while I weigh the alternatives. Will a radical change really work out better for me, for my children and, yes, for my spouse?

Before I make a decision, or take a step, I will redouble my efforts to apply the Al-Anon program. It could bring me to an entirely different, more constructive solution than the drastic ones I was considering.

"Make sure that the medicine you decide
on in a rash and desperate moment doesn't
turn out to be worse than the malady."

"It's a nice day," people say when the weather's fine. One of the things we learn in Al-Anon is that the kind of a day it is does not depend on the weather, but on our attitudes and reactions to what's happening.

We can make every day a nice day. Al-Anon's helpful little leaflet *"Just for Today"* says it this way: "Just for today I will be agreeable. I will look as well as I can, keep my voice low, be courteous. I won't find fault." This is bound to brighten the day, for me and everybody I meet!

Today's Reminder

I will make up my mind to be cheerful every waking moment of this day. I will not expect too much; this will shield me from being annoyed at little things that don't go just the way I wanted them to. I will try to accomplish something specific, perhaps some chore I have long been putting off. I will wear a pleasant smile for everyone I meet today.

> "What a comfortable feeling it gives me to realize that all I have to deal with is just this one day. It makes everything so much easier!"

When our problems enclose us and saturate our thoughts, we find ourselves in an isolation that gives us an acute sense of loneliness. We may confide in friends, but underneath we feel nobody understands what we are going through.

Dwelling on our troubles only shuts out a world that is waiting to be enjoyed. Nothing has real power to deprive us of the delights to be found in many daily experiences—even a routine household task, well done. For those of us who are fortunate enough to have young lives in our care, we can forget our troubles in devoting loving attention to them and their development. Observing our children is like reading a fascinating and often amusing book!

Today's Reminder

I may have big troubles but I can, if I will, make them less painful by turning my thoughts to happier things. I will not isolate myself in my problems. I will observe and enjoy what is good and pleasant in the world around me.

> "Let me not deprive myself of the many little joys that are mine for the taking."

The time has come for me to realize that my attitude, toward the life I am living and the people in it, can have a tangible, measurable effect on what happens to me day by day. If I am expectant of good, it will surely come to me. Even the grace of courtesy gives rich immediate rewards in warm response. Awareness of others—*a tolerant uncritical awareness*—will gradually change my personality for the better.

Today's Reminder

If I try each day to put my point of view and my attitudes on a sound spiritual basis, I know it will change all the circumstances of my life for the better, too. I will see the results in the way other people respond to me, and in the way my daily needs are met.

Concern, love and kindness on my part will be reflected in everything that takes place in my life.

> "Seek ye first the kingdom of God,
>   and all these things shall be added
>   unto you."
>
>   (*Matthew*)

What's the Big Idea in Al-Anon? What's behind these assurances that I *do* have the power to improve the shape and texture of my life?

It is this: *Look to yourself.* What am I doing that creates difficulties for me, or aggravates the ones I have? Could it be that I'm trying to fix everything by finding fault with somebody else? In Al-Anon I am encouraged to examine *my* impulses, motives, actions and words. This helps me to correct the causes of my own unease and not blame it on others.

Today's Reminder

At first, the idea that we might be at fault isn't easy to accept. We find it hard to believe that our behavior isn't all it should be.

Once I overcome the habit of justifying everything I do, and make use of such tools as courtesy, tenderness and a warm interest in others, miracles will happen. This I know, because I have seen them happen to others who tried the Al-Anon way.

"If you cannot make yourself what you would like to be, how can you expect to have another person exactly to your wishes? We want to see others perfect, yet our own faults go unattended."

(*Thomas A'Kempis—paraphrased*)

Some of us, after long enduring misfortunes we didn't know how to cope with, reached a breaking point. In our hopelessness we even felt rejected by God, so we never thought of turning to Him for help.

A wonderful thing about Al-Anon is that we are encouraged to renew our faith in a Power greater than ourselves. We may have thought we were beaten, but we had merely forgotten that God has given us the strength and the means to hold up our heads and live. We learn once more to identify ourselves with the Divine Principle that rules us all.

Today's Reminder

The sure knowledge that God is always with me, and expresses Himself through me, will guide me in every difficulty. This is the source of confidence and strength that will help me to face life in an entirely new way. His help will make possible a wholesome detachment from the problems that do not belong to me.

> "Let me add a spiritual dimension to my life; then I will never be alone in dealing with whatever troubles may appear."

So much of what there is to learn in Al-Anon has to do with discovering myself—the real person I am. One Greek philosopher said simply: "Know thyself"—another: "We would have inward peace, but will not look within."

Complete self-knowledge is impossible, but the "looking within" will open our eyes to many possible improvements. It is difficult because we're afraid we won't like what we see, and we may have misgivings about being able to change ourselves. Yet what we may find when we look within may be quite a surprise package—all those many good qualities tucked away under heavy layers of guilt.

Today's Reminder

Our greatest handicap is self-deception. We cannot recognize in ourselves the faults we criticize in others.

If I could only foresee what an inspiring experience it is to search out the real *me*, I would not hesitate. The first step, after all, is to be completely honest in our search.

> "If I knew what I was really like,
> chances are I'd like myself much
> better than I do."

Have I been trying to live the Al-Anon program? Then I must surely be learning to overcome any tendency to control others—the directing, scheming and manipulating that can only result in my own defeat.

I will not interfere with the activities of the alcoholic, or watch over him, counsel him, or assume his responsibilities. He must have the same freedom to make his own decisions as I have, since he must suffer for them if they are wrong.

Perhaps I have felt I had a right and an obligation to set the standards for the family and compel those around me to live up to them. In Al-Anon we learn a better way.

Here is a vivid picture, from the great novelist Tolstoy, which makes the situation clear:

Today's Reminder

"I sit on a man's back, choking him and making him carry me, and yet assure myself and others that I am very sorry for him and wish to ease his lot by all possible means—*except by getting off his back.*"

> "Teach me to leave to others their
> inborn right to dignity and independence,
> as I wish to have them leave mine to me."

We do not come to Al-Anon—or should not —to look for pity. We should not expect the other members to assure us that our resentments are justified, or that we ought to take aggressive action. Indeed, we learn to resist aggression from others by maintaining our dignity and poise. In short, what the Al-Anon program does for us, through its members, is to help us *change the way we look at* our family problems.

If I complain about something "he" did, somebody may point out that I seem too determined. (I will not even take it amiss if the word is "stubborn"!) When I reveal that I am checking up on his activities, I may be told that my interference won't help matters, but will keep me from growing.

Today's Reminder

Al-Anon meetings and friendships can be inspiring, interesting, enlightening, and even fun. But they are also dedicated to the serious business of making me into a confident, spiritually-oriented adult human being. If that is what I want, I will listen with an open mind, accept suggestions and put to good use what I learn.

> "I pray to let nothing stand in the way of my being receptive to what Al-Anon has to offer."

We who have chosen our life partners from the ranks of alcoholics often feel our lives are especially difficult and complicated. And they often are. We come to believe, quite mistakenly, that we're the only people in the world with real trouble! Let us recognize that the alcoholic—insecure, lonely, and often too sensitive to life's realities—usually has many endearing qualities to be grateful for. Indeed, many of us wouldn't want to exchange him for a less interesting, if more dependable partner.

Yet matters may have reached the point of desperation and we are completely hopeless. What to do?

Today's Reminder

In Al-Anon I discover in myself the power to throw new light on a seemingly hopeless situation. I learn I must use this power, not to change the alcoholic over whom I am powerless, but to overcome my own distorted ideas and attitudes. If I can bring sunshine into our home, it cannot fail to affect those in it.

> "Help me to use the gifts You have
> given me. I want to use them to
> help others through making my
> own world better and brighter."

Here's an eye-opening, *mind*-opening question to ask myself: What am I doing with what I've got? Instead of crying over what I don't have, and wishing my life were different, *what am I doing with what I've got?*

Am I so sure I'm doing everything possible to make my life a success? Am I using my capabilities well? Do I recognize and appreciate all I have to be grateful for?

Actually I am the possessor of unlimited resources. The more I do with them, the more they will grow, to overshadow and cancel out the difficult and painful aspects that now get so much of my attention.

Today's Reminder

Isn't my life full of potential good that I'm not using? Couldn't I bring it to fruition by changing my attitude? As a beginning, I will apply liberal amounts of gratitude for even my littlest advantages and pleasures. When I build on this precious foundation of present, tangible good, things will continue to change for the better.

> "God make me grateful for all the good things I have been taking for granted."

Again I ask myself the same question as yesterday's: "What am I doing with what I have?" This query can be applied in many ways. Take, for instance, the faculty of being able to remember. If I have been given the gift of a good, clear memory, how do I use it?

It isn't likely that God conferred this gift on me for the purpose of dredging up old wrongs, injured feelings, futile regrets and personal sufferings. That would clearly be a misuse of His gift, when everyone has so many pleasant and satisfying things to remember.

Today's Reminder

What am I doing with this precious ability to recall what happened in the past? If I use it to remember enjoyments and interesting experiences, it will give me a saving perspective on the problems I am encountering in the here and now. I can also use the gift of memory for storing up today's blessings to tide me over future woes.

> "Let not thy thoughts dwell upon the
> days of thy sorrows, but rather on
> those which brought thee brightness
> and peace."

Occasionally an Al-Anon meeting dredges up grievances and reports of domestic hostility. The chairman of one such meeting, having also told about "family fights" of her own, jolted the group with this final comment:

"I've often wondered, when I start a battle with my husband, how I'd feel if somebody were making a tape recording of what I was saying, and the tone of voice I was using to say it. I'd be screeching and shouting like a fishwife; I'd bring up all my weapons of sarcasm and lash out. And by the way, the word *sarcasm* comes from a Greek word meaning *to tear flesh.*

"Wouldn't I feel pretty cheap if I could *hear myself* being played back? Wouldn't it give me some idea of my part in the family troubles?

"Please, please, let's *listen to ourselves* and see if it doesn't help us to cool off."

Today's Reminder

I will, from now on, take note of how disagreements start in my home. If I am the instigator, this is the first thing I will try to correct in myself. If I am challenged by an angry person, I will respond quietly, or not at all.

> "A soft answer turneth away wrath,
>   but grievous words stir up anger."
>
> (Proverbs)

When an Al-Anon member undertakes to give advice, it is important to remember that it should be limited to *helping the other person in terms of spiritual growth*. There is danger in going beyond this and advising *action to be taken*. None of us have the right to do this.

Sometimes a frustrated neurotic gives advice that stirs up hostility between a man and wife. She may make the situation much worse by justifying the wife's resentment. Promoting such resentments can have serious consequences. So, too, can urging her to "stand up for her rights" or "not to allow this or that." She is getting unconscious satisfaction from managing other people's lives, while she imagines her intentions are only good.

Today's Reminder

Heaven protect me from my good friends who, with only the best intentions, keep the wounds of my resentment open, weaken me by their pity, and justify my complaints. In the name of doing good, they can hamper my restoring a tolerant and loving relationship with my family.

> "We must not be easy in giving credit
> to every word and suggestion, but
> carefully and leisurely weigh the
> matter according to God."
> *(Thomas A'Kempis)*

Once upon a time there was a married couple who lived in a beautiful house, and had lots of the material things that many of us think are important to contentment. They were not contented, however. What with one little misunderstanding and another, the situation grew worse. Nobody would give way an inch in their bitter arguments, until at last their love turned to hate. Finally the wife insisted that the inside of the house be divided by a brick wall, behind which each could live in his and her own quarters. Each went his own way, and they never spoke to each other again as long as they lived. They had many wretched years in their isolation.

* * *

Am I unknowingly building a wall between myself and the person I married? Is it being made of stubbornness, self-will, self-righteousness and a desire to punish? Such a wall can be as hard and unyielding as though it were made of real bricks. It would leave me no space in which to grow. As one member put it:

> "God grant me the wisdom to recognize
> the faults I am building into a wall,
> such a wall as cannot be penetrated
> even by love."

We hear it over and over again, in both AA and Al-Anon: this program is *spiritual, not religious*. Each of us must find our own way to Heaven and the Al-Anon teachings reinforce our faith in the way we choose to worship, whatever it may be. If our dedicated practice of Al-Anon helps us make a Heaven on earth, no religious faith would quarrel with this happy outcome.

Yet sometimes a member, devoted to a particular religion, may try to win others over to her faith, virtuously convinced that she is only trying to help. This can lead to confusion and many difficulties, and may indeed result in creating a rift in a marriage whose foundation is a common faith.

Today's Reminder

It is emphasized in our Traditions and in much of our literature that a) we are not affiliated with any other organization, and b) that the tenets of any faith can be applied with the Al-Anon program.

> "I pray for the wisdom not to involve
> myself with the personal lives and
> beliefs of others, and to help them
> only by means of Al-Anon principles."

A good way to "get out from under" some of our daily problems is to stop *reacting* to everything that occurs. Some of us have a constant drive to *do something* about everything that happens, everything that someone says to us.

There is a time to act, of course. But the action should be based on careful thinking out of the factors. It should not be triggered by every wind that blows. When something displeases us, it isn't a threat to our lives, our safety, or anything important. If we keep it in perspective, it will help us to "let it go."

Today's Reminder

I will try to overcome my tendency to react to what people say or do. I can't know why they do it, because I cannot understand their inner unhappiness and compulsions, any more than they can understand mine. When I *react*, I put the control of my peace of mind in the hands of others. My serenity is under *my* control, and I will not relinquish it for trivial occurrences.

> "I pray for the tolerance and
> the wisdom to avoid reacting
> to what other people say and do."

A member speaks in a meeting: "I keep trying to get my point across to him but nothing I say seems to penetrate."

Another member answers: "Perhaps when we can't get our views across to the alcoholic, or anyone else, it is time to consider whether the point we are trying to make is really valid. Could it be that it isn't right or reasonable or that our determination to 'get the point across' is being used at the wrong time? Are we making allowances for the other person's right to a different point of view?"

Today's Reminder

Right and wrong are not always black and white. Before I take a positive stand, it would be wise first to make sure that it is reasonable, and then that I have taken into account all possible reasons against my "right" point of view. An open mind is a handy thing to have when once I become willing to *Live and Let Live*.

> "Let me not force my own certainties
> on others. I could be wrong. A
> generous tolerance can smooth out
> many rough places in my day-to-
> day living."

We often hear it said in Al-Anon that the Twelve Steps are a way of life, not only in coping with the problems of alcoholism, but in everything else. We have only to replace the word "alcohol" with the name of the problem which confronts us.

The beginning of Step One, for example, says: "Admitted we were powerless over *alcohol.*" That admission can apply to many other difficulties we feel we should be able to control, but are not.

I do have a power, a God-given one, and that is power over my own mind, emotions and reactions. If I exercise that power wisely, the problems outside of me will work out without my interference.

Today's Reminder

Before Al-Anon, I did everything I could think of to manage the life of my spouse. Yet I was demonstrating every day that I could not even manage my own! I felt I was being forced into doing and being what I did not want to do and be. In Al-Anon I discovered how to be myself.

> "If I try to govern another person's life,
> I will fail. When I fix my thoughts
> on improving my own I can count on
> the help of my Higher Power."

Most of us, when we first come into Al-Anon, have but one idea: sobriety for the alcoholic. We learn at once that this is not Al-Anon's purpose. We have ourselves to change and, by great good fortune, the changes we make can so improve the environment we live in that the alcoholic will seek sobriety.

We may think all our problems have been solved when the alcoholic is safely in AA, so we feel we can rest on our oars. Meetings and telephone talks with our Al-Anon friends don't seem so necessary. This is due to forgetting two basic truths:

Today's Reminder

1. Emotional disturbance is one cause of alcoholism. This condition can improve as the alcoholic practices the spiritual elements of the AA program. The adjustment period may be long— and trying to our patience unless we have Al-Anon to help us grow, too.

2. What we have learned in Al-Anon, and all the help we have received, must be passed along to troubled newcomers in the fellowship we embraced when we were in trouble.

> "If I believe that life will be rich
> and rewarding only as I live it with
> spiritual guidelines, I know I will
> always need Al-Anon."

An Al-Anon member with a particularly serious problem was told by another at a meeting: "I just wouldn't put up with it!"

The answer came: "I am not, as you say, putting up with it. I am trying to correct my own faults, keep my mouth shut when I am tempted to yell and scream at him, and keep hands off his problems. You see, I never want to forget that I have a commitment to my husband. I want to live up to that commitment which I made, willingly and solemnly, when I married him."

Today's Reminder

Any marriage made in expectation of lifelong bliss and freedom from care is bound to bring us to some shocking realizations that life just isn't like that. An adult point of view recognizes that alcoholism and its train of troubles is only one of the disasters that can happen to a marriage. We would face others with courage; why not this? The commitment to the person we married demands that we do everything we can to correct our problems. *What to do* we learn in Al-Anon. How *we* use it is up to us.

". . . in sickness and in health, for better or for worse . . ."

If irrational and irresponsible behavior on the part of the alcoholic has betrayed us into assuming an attitude of contempt for him, some serious examination of ourselves is in order.

They are not "bad boys," who must be directed, disciplined or punished by us. They are sick, confused and guilt-ridden human beings with badly battered egos.

God has given no one the right to humiliate another. In every one of His children there are qualities that should command our respect, and to withhold it is a wrong that will return to wound us.

Today's Reminder

It is vital to my serenity to separate, in my mind, the sickness of alcoholism from the person who suffers from it. I will dignify him with the respect which is everyone's due. This, in turn, will give him back the self-esteem that is an important element in wanting sobriety.

> "The surest plan to make a Man
> Is: *Think him so.*"
>
> (*James R. Lowell*)

Until I understand the inner meaning of the Twelve Steps, my natural impulse is to resist admitting that they apply to me.

I don't *want* to believe I am powerless over alcohol, or that I have allowed my life to become unmanageable. Yet I know I must accept the First Step before I can make progress.

Although most of us do acknowledge a Power greater than ourselves, we are shocked at first by the idea that we need to be "restored to sanity," as the Second Step suggests. Yet an honest appraisal of many of my reactions shows me I have too often resorted to futile and childish tricks to achieve what I wanted. With my thoughts distorted by fear, despair and resentment, and my nerves overwrought, I could not think clearly nor make wise decisions.

Today's Reminder

Each of the Twelve Steps challenges me to be absolutely honest with myself. They will make me ready to accept the help of my Higher Power in restoring myself to the wholesome sanity of a mature, reasonable adult.

> "The Twelve Steps will point a way to
> God and His infinite wisdom, by which
> I hope always to be guided."

When I concentrate on little things that annoy me, and they sprout resentments that grow bigger and bigger, I seem to forget how I could be "stretching" my world and broadening my perspective. That's the way to shrink troubles down to their real size.

Worrying about trifles saps my spiritual energy which I could certainly put to better use. Am I willing to waste my life in this way?

When something or somebody is giving me trouble, let me see the incident *in relation to the rest of my life,* especially the part that is good, and for which I should be grateful. A wider view of my circumstances will make me better able to deal with all difficulties, big and little.

Today's Reminder

I refuse to let my serenity be drowned out by happenings that are in themselves unimportant. I will not be made uneasy by what others do, whether they intend to hurt me or not. I will not clutter up my thoughts with resentment; it would not profit me but, worse, it would hurt me.

> "Why do we accept things that trouble us, when we could do something about them?"

One of our delusions is that we, as spouses of alcoholics, are "running the show." This form of self-deception can only increase our frustrations. It makes the home a battleground in which the alcoholic has the best chance of winning every encounter. We are often out-witted by the alcoholic's lightning changes of mood, his promises, challenges and other maneuvers. This is the best reason for detach-ing our minds and our emotions from the minute-by-minute conflict, and seeking a peaceful, orderly way of life within ourselves. If we stop fighting out every incident that happens, absence of an active adversary is bound to bring about wholesome changes in the home environment, and everyone in it.

Today's Reminder

I will not try to outwit or out-maneuver anyone else, but will proceed quietly to live my life so I will have less reason for self-reproach. I will with-draw my mind from what others do, and think of what I am doing. I will not *react* to challenging words and actions.

> "When you are offended at any
> man's fault, turn to yourself
> and study your own failings.
> Then you will forget your anger."
> (*Epictetus*)

After we have been trying to use the Al-Anon program for a while, one thing becomes clear: *we can get unlimited benefits from changing our way of thinking.* No realistic, reasonable person would consider this an easy task; indeed, there is nothing more difficult in life!

Suppose, just suppose, we were resolved to follow this one idea, expressed by one of AA's founders in an informal talk:

"Let's stop throwing blame around." This one idea could be explored, meditated on, *acted upon,* from now until the end of our days. What would happen if we *stopped blaming anyone for anything?* We would experience miracles of tolerance and grace—rich spiritual rewards, reflected in a life of real fulfillment.

Today's Reminder

I will try not to blame the alcoholic. How can I know what he is going through in his struggle with the bottle, the ever-present escape? What can I know of his strivings to improve after he is sober? I will not blame him. I will not blame anybody. I will not blame myself.

> "Who is to blame? Whom have I the right
> to blame? Let me concentrate on keeping
> my own conduct from being at fault;
> more I cannot do."

Even when I find myself growing in understanding of Al-Anon, and can see tangible results from my new attitudes, I might question such a statement as this:

"Al-Anon is a way to personal freedom."

Enmeshed in a difficult family situation, we doubt we can ever be free from all this woe and care. When we think how closely our lives are intertwined with others, we're sure that personal freedom is impossible.

The key word is *personal*. We *can* free ourselves from many involvements that *seem* necessary. In Al-Anon we can learn to develop our own personalities, to reinforce our personal freedom by leaving others free to control their actions and destinies.

Today's Reminder

Personal freedom is mine for the taking. No matter how close are the ties of love and concern that bind me to my family and friends, I must always remember that I am an individual, free to be myself and live my own life in serenity and joy.

> "When I know I am free within myself,
> I will be better able to give loving
> thought to others."

Today let's review some of the sayings of an Al-Anon founder:

"Smugness is the very worst sin of all, I believe. It is difficult for a shaft of light to pierce the armor of self-righteousness."

"Many of the things I thought I did unselfishly turned out to be pure rationalizations to get my own way about something. This disclosure doubled my urge to live by the Twelve Steps as thoroughly as I could."

"In the early days I was deeply hurt that someone else had brought my husband to sobriety, when I could not. Now I have learned that a wife can rarely, if ever, do this job. I found no peace of mind until I recognized this fact."

"The word 'humbly' was one I never understood. It used to seem servile. Today it means seeing myself in true relation to my fellowman and to God."

Today's Reminder

"It is easy to fool oneself about motives, and admitting it is hard, but very beneficial."

> "Bargaining with God and asking
> Him to grant my wishes is not
> the highest form of prayer. It
> is very different from praying
> only for knowledge of God's will
> for me. . . ."

An early Al-Anon member once said:

"I tried to manage my husband's life, although not even able to manage my own. I wanted to get inside his brain and turn the screws in what I thought was the right direction. It took me a long time to realize that this was not my job..I just wasn't equipped for it. None of us are. So I began to turn the screws *in my own head* in the right direction. This has taught me a little more about managing my own life."

Today's Reminder

If my life has become unmanageable, how can I get control of it? Am I being forced into doing things I don't want to do, like losing my temper, contriving, conniving and scheming to make things work out the way I want them? Am I now the kind of person I really want to be? An honest effort to manage my own life will open many doors to me that my distorted thinking had kept closed.

"If thou canst not make *thyself* such
a one as thou wouldst, how canst thou
expect to have another according to
thy liking?"

(*Thomas A'Kempis*)

One reason we go to Al-Anon is to learn about alcoholism. We learn that it is an illness which could end in physical, mental and spiritual bankruptcy. We also learn that there is no known cure, but that sobriety is possible through the healing help of AA—*when the alcoholic is ready*. We learn that our own reactions to the alcoholic situation have not been reasonable; we, too, went downhill. We learn that an honest appraisal of ourselves will open the way to improvement and start us on the upward climb to sanity and serenity. Reading Al-Anon literature and exchanging experiences and ideas with our Al-Anon friends will give us strong support in this effort.

Today's Reminder

To live the Al-Anon way can lead to such contentment as we have never before experienced. To those of us who earnestly use the program, it offers the richest of benefits. It is a learning process that works best for those who approach it with willingness and humility.

> "I ask God to make me willing to
> learn how to live more fully,
> through the light which I can
> find in Al-Anon."

Someone suggested we add another slogan to those we use in Al-Anon: *Listen and learn.* My first reaction was: "No! Not everybody at an Al-Anon meeting says something that is helpful. What about those who advise: 'Throw the bum out!' Doesn't that negate everything we're supposed to hear in Al-Anon?" But wait! What I learn from the negative comments can be useful in opening my mind to my own wrong thinking. When someone gives advice, I can say to myself: "But we're not supposed to advise in Al-Anon." If someone expresses hostility and resentment for what the alcoholic does, it can teach me to avoid those very things in myself.

Today's Reminder

Listen and learn is sound doctrine, if we use it well. We don't make significant progress in our thinking if we're only listening to ourselves talk.

"It is the disease of not listening . . . that I am troubled with."

(*William Shakespeare*)

"I pray that I may learn from listening—whether or not I agree with what I hear."

Once there was a man whose beloved wife was transformed from the charming girl he had married, into a sodden drunkard. She suffered from a disease called alcoholism, although neither of them knew it.

He was always angry and frustrated because he couldn't make her stop drinking. The more he tried, the worse she felt about it, and the more she drank. She was full of guilt and self-reproach because she left everything to him. He had to get the children ready for school, do the shopping, cook meals and clean house.

Then one day somebody told him about Al-Anon. Although he knew his case was hopeless, he thought he'd try it anyway. As he read, and asked questions and listened at meetings, he found he could get some perspective on his problems. When he learned his wife had a disease, compulsive drinking, he stopped blaming himself for not being able to control her. He realized the children resented him because he was often cross and unreasonable, and that they loved mama because she never scolded and they knew instinctively she was sick. He began to consider his own needs, for rest, quiet and a bit of recreation, and arranged to have a housekeeper take over the home chores. He made many changes, but especially in his attitude toward the alcoholic.

After a spell of rebellion and resistance, she saw that she would have to get help.

One day she asked him to take her to an AA meeting.

In Al-Anon we often speak of the importance of prayer. This idea calls for some reflection. If I could get what I pray for, would it really make me happy? Do I always know what is best for me? Do I bargain with the God I pray to: ("I want my spouse, but only if he or she will stop drinking.") or give Him instructions: ("Please don't let Bill keep on drinking!")

Today's Reminder

One thing must ultimately be accepted: few of us know what we really want, and none of us knows what is best for us. That knowledge remains, in spite of all our determined resistance, in the hands of God.

This is the reason for limiting our prayers to requests for guidance, an open mind to receive it, and the fortitude to act upon it.

I will quietly defer any decisions until my contact with God has made me certain they are right for me. And I will pray to be kept from taking any action, even a little one, *that is intended to punish another.*

> "Every good gift and every perfect gift
> is from above and cometh down from the
> Father of lights with Whom is no
> variableness, neither shadow of turning."
> (*General Epistle of James*)

This is the story of a newcomer to Al-Anon who was not a newcomer . . . certainly not a novice, for she had the courage to break out of a situation that was hampering her work in the program.

Seeing a new face at the meeting, the chairman asked her to tell about herself. Instead of launching into a recital of her domestic problems (which turned out to be quite severe)—she told what had made her leave the group where she'd started some months before.

"Quite frankly," she said, "I'm shopping around for a group I can feel comfortable in. I grabbed Al-Anon like a life-preserver, which it certainly is for me. I joined a group, never missed meetings, and read Al-Anon literature every day. That's how I got the idea that everybody in a group, and everyone in the fellowship, too, are equals. The group I belonged to was *run*—and I DO mean run, by a managing old-timer who ruled everything with an iron hand. She'd been secretary for eight years, chaired the meetings, decided on the programs. She knew what was good for us, all right! We didn't even have to think for ourselves. And I couldn't see that anybody was making much progress—the membership was what you might call a shifting population. Most of them just gave up on Al-Anon—and all because of this one person. I didn't give up, so here I am, hoping for a group where I can really see the Al-Anon fellowship in action."

Cheery platitudes are not much help to new-comers in really desperate straits. Nor is the hearty attitude: "Come on, snap out of it—Al-Anon will work wonders for you!"

A wife and mother who has seen everything go down the drain, who has lived through losing her home, going on public relief, with the husband in an institution or a prison, may feel even farther removed from hope in a bright, optimistic circle of Al-Anon people who are on the way up.

Such newcomers should select sponsors who can understand their problems and help them, with patience and tact, to meet the challenge.

Today's Reminder

It is a spiritual experience to lead a desperate newcomer into a new point of view. We learn the subtle difference between pity and sympathetic understanding. We do not flaunt our own success in Al-Anon; we let it speak for itself.

A good sponsor keeps in touch, gently conveys the idea that it's always darkest just before dawn, and gives a lift to the bruised ego.

> "I pray for the opportunity to help the hopeless; it will show me the way to share myself with someone in great need."

Heard at an Al-Anon meeting:

"I have only one person's guilt to carry: my own. If the alcoholic blames me for his difficulties, I will not accept that blame, but I will not defend myself, either, for that would only start a fruitless battle. I know he blames me because of his painful need to unload some of his remorse on somebody else. This should generate only compassion in me—not resentment or anger."

Another member responds: "I wish I could believe that! When my husband gets through telling me off I feel as though the devil were sitting on my back with a fifty pound lead weight in each pocket!"

Today's Reminder

There is no need for me to accept blame for another person's irrational actions. I will deal with my own shortcomings. If I do this honestly—following the Fourth to Tenth Steps—the change in me will be reflected in every person whose life touches mine.

"Let me weigh my misdeeds on an honest
scale and make restitution as well as
I can. But let not the scale be un-
balanced by the weight of what
others have done."

When I say the Serenity Prayer, over and over again, I could fall into the habit of merely parroting the words without being aware of their meaning. This would blunt one of my most useful Al-Anon tools. If I *think* of the meaning of each phrase as I say it, my understanding will grow and along with it my capability to realize *the difference between what I can change, and what I cannot.*

The prayer states first that there are elements in my life which I have no power to change; my serenity depends upon my accepting them. The more I fight them, the more they will torment me. "Courage to change the things I can" gives me unlimited freedom to work on those elements which *are* my concern.

Today's Reminder

The Serenity Prayer suggests I ask God "for courage to change the *things* I can." The word is *things,* not *people.* True, there is much room for improvement in my life, but it can come only from changing my own attitudes and actions for the better.

> "In every problem, great and small,
> the Serenity Prayer will
> work for me if I keep aware of
> its meaning every time I say it."

Sometimes it happens that a member at a meeting "talks good Al-Anon" but those who know her well are aware that it is only skin-deep. She professes compassion for the alcoholic, but all the softness goes out the window when she is crossed or disappointed or annoyed. The real, untamed faults come through, and she hardly even realizes it herself.

When we make only superficial changes in ourselves, and give only ardent lip-service to the program, our progress is slow and our relapses many. The regeneration must be a true spiritual rebirth. It must go very deep, with each character flaw replaced by a new and good quality.

Today's Reminder

I must be completely honest with myself in uncovering the faults which hamper my spiritual growth. One by one, watchfully and painstakingly, I will replace them with constructive attitudes.

> "Men imagine they communicate their
> virtue . . . only by overt actions and
> words. They do not see that virtue
> or its opposite emits a breath at
> every moment."
> (Emerson: *Essay on Self-Reliance—paraphrased*)

Heard at an Al-Anon meeting:

"Before I came to Al-Anon, it was like groping around in a dark room, trying to sidestep the obstacles without being able to see them. Because there was no light, I was constantly getting hurt because I tripped over things, or bumped into them.

"Then I came into Al-Anon and learned that I have the power *to turn on the light,* to get a clear view of my life, its difficulties and good things. Often I still forget to turn on the light. I still hurt myself. But I'm getting better as I do more reading and living the program."

Today's Reminder

Looking for light on a grim situation? Here it is, in Al-Anon. Nobody can force you to accept it, but you'll want to when you learn how much easier it can become to deal with life's inevitable problems. As one member put it: "I see things differently now."

". . . and God said: Let there be Light. . . ."
(*Genesis*)
". . . light always dispels the darkness."

When I hear it said in an Al-Anon meeting that I can help myself, no matter how great my burdens and troubles are, I may think: "Easy to say, but you don't know what *I'm* going through."

Applying a little sensible realism to this, let me ask myself whether I'm not building up trifles into monstrosities that *seem* unbearable. Most of us do, at some time or other. We may magnify disagreements about money for instance; we expand minor slights into huge grievances. Without realizing it, we're looking for trouble and are ready to fasten on little things that we could easily pass over if we really wanted our own peace of mind.

Today's Reminder

If I don't make big problems out of little ones, I can save myself much grief. Fighting for my "rights" often creates more difficulty than accepting less than I expect. If I really value my serenity, I will avoid making big issues out of trifles. Giving in and letting go becomes easier as I practice it, and it pays big dividends in inner satisfaction.

> "Whensoever a man desires anything
> inordinately, he is presently
> disquieted within himself."
> (*Thomas A'Kempis*)

When we speak of miracles happening in Al-Anon, we often include among these the entry of a spouse into AA and sobriety.

This is indeed a miracle, but it is not *our* miracle; it is the alcoholic's. It is not our business (nor has it ever been!) to watch over him, worry about his sobriety, see that he doesn't drink, that he goes to the right number of AA meetings. If we continue the techniques of management and supervision that did so much to make a mess of life during the drinking days, we're headed for trouble.

We can and should be grateful on his behalf, but our business is with Al-Anon and ourselves. This wonderful program will help us make something of our own lives. Our responsibility to the alcoholic is to let him manage his own sobriety, and to be gentle, courteous and cooperative.

Today's Reminder

The AA member, however close to me, is the concern of his friends in AA. He must be left free to follow the program in his own way. If I am truly grateful, I will keep hands off.

"Study to be quiet, and to do your own
  business."   (*Thessalonians*)
". . . and confuse not the business of others
  with your own."

Without faith in a power greater than myself, I am like a storm-tossed ship without a rudder. I am flung from one trouble to another; however bravely I may battle the elements, my own strength and wisdom are not enough.

All of us need something to cling to with absolute confidence. If I have been disillusioned by disappointments, or have been let down by someone I trusted, it makes me feel as though I were alone and vulnerable in a hostile world.

I will not deprive myself of God's help and guidance. I see it at work in Al-Anon as we share knowledge, courage and hope with each other. Confidence and dignity are restored to us by the knowledge that we are God's children.

Today's Reminder

If my faith has been dimmed by disappointment, I can begin to regain it by clinging to a spiritual idea like the one expressed in the Serenity Prayer. This living philosophy will give me a secure foundation of faith.

"For we walk by faith, not by sight. . . ."
(*Second Corinthians*)

The wife with a long-standing habit of managing her husband may not even realize that she is constantly directing and admonishing him:

"Don't wear that blue shirt today—wear this one."—"It's almost time for church—you'd better get ready."—"Don't take the car out in this weather!"—"You've made four AA meetings this week and the kitchen needs painting."

Trifles, yes, but such an attitude deprives the husband of all freedom of choice, all dignity and manhood. She plays the mother role and treats him like a child who wouldn't know what to do without being told.

Today's Reminder

If in the troubled drinking years I unwisely assumed responsibility that should have been my husband's, I will now break these habits of managing. I realize now, through Al-Anon, that sobriety might have come much sooner if I had been able to stand aside and let the alcoholic suffer the consequences of his own choices. I will respect his rights as an individual.

> "Each of us has the right and the
> obligation to make our own decisions.
> It is character-destroying to usurp
> that right."

Once upon a time there was an Enormous Thumb belonging to a woman with an Alcoholic Husband and Three Teenaged Children.

The four of them lived under her thumb, so of course they couldn't do much growing up. Often their spirits writhed under the weight; every time they tried to get out from under, they'd do something wrong and the thumb would clamp down on them again.

Father managed by keeping himself flattened out drunk most of the time; he was so cute about escaping to a bottle that, no matter how much mama watched, she couldn't catch him at it until he'd drunk himself into unconsciousness. Everyone thought she was a Very Nice Lady, and they were sorry she was having such a hard time with her family.

There was really no reason for her to come to Al-Anon to solve her problems because she always knew just what to do about everything. But she did want to make her husband stop drinking, so she thought she'd try it. She was quite unhappy at first because some of the members were not inclined to Pull any Punches. She was quite indignant when they tried to show her what she was doing to her family, but to everyone's amazement the Thumb began to shrink and lose weight, and things looked brighter.

More and more she realized what she was doing and, being a Determined Character, she applied the program every day and her other problems took care of themselves very nicely.

We come together in an Al-Anon group for the purpose of sharing experience, strength and hope with each other. This we do by attending meetings, discussing, listening, counseling, telephoning each other for comfort and renewal of confidence.

It is wonderful to know that this close communication, this keeping in touch, is not limited to the members of a single group; it embraces the whole world! This message came to the United States from the publication of the Al-Anon groups of South Africa:

Today's Reminder

"Learn to face things as they come, and when they come, with calm deliberation. We may not be able to control events, but we can control our attitudes toward them."

This clear message from a faraway continent will inspire Al-Anon people everywhere in their search for serenity. It demonstrates how closely akin we are in our loving fellowship.

> "And be renewed in the spirit of your
> mind . . . for we are members one of
> another."
>
> (*Ephesians*)

We come to Al-Anon because we believe it has something we want. In other words, we come to *get* something for ourselves. At first we have no idea that this *getting* is intimately involved with *giving*.

We soon discover that our willingness to help others has an immediate and beneficent reaction on us. Our progress in the program depends on that satisfying sense of sharing, giving of ourselves, whether it be to enlighten and comfort a newcomer, serving as a group officer, supporting our fellowship or listening patiently to someone in trouble.

Today's Reminder

The more I give of myself and the more generously I open my heart and my mind to others, the more growth I will experience as I deal with my problems. I learn in Al-Anon never to measure my *giving* against my *getting;* the very giving provides my reward.

> "The giver is only a channel for the gifts he has received from God. He cannot hoard or withhold them without blocking the channel."

The new member of a group is understandably upset, distraught and perhaps even desperate. Just as ours did in the beginning, her trials seem too great for a human being to endure. She is not yet aware that she may be making it worse by complaining, weeping and trying to outwit the alcoholic. All these things we learn *not* to do after we've been in Al-Anon for a time. Her recital may even be distorted by hysteria—this is natural, too.

All this should warn us not to make sweeping judgments on anyone else's problem, or suggest making any decisions for her. We must help her become able to make them for herself.

Today's Reminder

No matter how unbearable a person's situation appears, I know I am not capable of judging it, since I can't possibly know all the factors involved. Nor can I measure another's emotional pain by my own experience and feelings. But I *can* offer comfort and hope, and the healing therapy of the Al-Anon program.

> Our Eighth Tradition says: "Al-Anon
> Twelfth Step work should remain
> forever *non-professional*."

All kinds of people turn to Al-Anon for help—rich and poor, educated and un-schooled, people with social polish and people without.

Sometimes it may be observed that those who have had more advantages tend to be a little patronizing of others; they may criticize faulty grammar or poor speech or inappropriate clothing.

It is fortunate that those with the illusion of superiority *have* come to Al-Anon, for they will find out that it is a *fellowship of equals*. It often happens that a person from whom they least expect spiritual insight will make a statement that reaches directly to the heart of the hearers, to give light and comfort and hope.

Today's Reminder

I am in Al-Anon to help myself solve my problems, to overcome my shortcomings, and to help others find serenity just as I am trying to find it. I will make no personal judgments nor criticisms, but will humbly accept the good in everything I find in the fellowship.

> "Who am I to judge God's children by their manner of speaking or by what they wear? I will listen for the help they can give me."

The Twelve Steps make up a body of spiritual wisdom that unfolds and expands our understanding as we study them, one after another. There is one Step, however, that could be studied from the very outset, every day, for its extraordinary power to throw light on the others. This is the Eleventh, which speaks of prayer and meditation.

Meditation is the quiet and sustained application of the mind to the contemplation of a *spiritual truth*. Its purpose is to *deflect* our minds from the problems we are experiencing, to raise our thoughts above the grievances and discontent that color our thinking.

Today's Reminder

I will set aside at least five minutes, morning and night, for spiritual concentration, excluding from my mind all but one spiritual idea. I will begin and end each meditation with a conscious awareness of God.

> "Sought through prayer and meditation
> to improve our conscious contact with
> God as we understood Him, praying only
> for knowledge of His will for us and
> the power to carry that out."
> (*Step Eleven of the Twelve*)

A brief study of some intangibles:

Our attitudes are usually conveyed to other people by what we say and do—and how. *If the attitudes really reflect what we feel.* Gentle actions and soft, courteous words may only counterfeit our true feelings. We may even *think* we have overcome resentment, self-righteousness and self-pity, but if they are still there inside us, they will in some mysterious way emanate from us and deny what we try to convey by our play-acting.

"How can he tell?" asks a confused wife. "I never raise my voice, never argue, try to do what he expects, and yet he's always challenging me!"

Today's Reminder

Merely to change my behavior, and what I say and do, does not prove a change of inward attitude. I am deceiving myself if I imagine I can completely disguise my real feelings. They will somehow come through, and prolong the hostility in my family. I must root out entirely the troublesome emotions I've been trying to hide.

> "There are more things in heaven and earth. . . . than are dreamt of in your philosophy."
>
> (*William Shakespeare*)

In the great Spanish classic *Don Quixote*, the author tells about a bemused hero who goes forth to right the world's wrongs. Among his adventures he has an encounter with some windmills that he imagines to be menacing giants. He fights them with his rusty sword until he falls exhausted.

Don't we, too, often wear ourselves out "tilting at windmills"—using our heavy artillery of anger and worry over trifling annoyances that aren't worth all that futile struggle?

Today's Reminder

Do I waste my time and energy fighting situations that are actually not worth a second thought? I will not allow my imagination to build small troubles into big ones. I will try to see each situation clearly, and give it only the value and attention it deserves. This is the sanity to which I want to be restored, as the Second Step suggests.

> "God grant me the sense of proportion
> to judge the difference between an
> incident and a crisis."

Our Slogans are so clear and simple, yet they may still mean different things to different people. We naturally color them somewhat, according to our own experience and reaction to the words and ideas.

For example, the slogan *Let Go and Let God* may suggest to some people that all we have to do is sidestep the challenges that confront us and somehow, by a kind of spiritual magic, God will do all the work.

There was a purpose in His giving His children free will, intelligence and good sense; we can fulfill ourselves only by *using* these gifts in dealing with the daily problems that arise.

Today's Reminder

I may be ready to submit to God's guidance, I may humbly ask for it, but along with being willing, I must cooperate by doing my part. If I am truly receptive, He will make His will known to me step by step, each day; *but I must carry it out.*

"Surrender to God's will does not give us a passport to inertia. Each of us must try to carry out God's will, which He transmits to us in ways we recognize only after we have made ourselves willing and aware."

One suggestion we hear in Al-Anon is: *Don't take anyone's inventory but your own.* This may surprise us, if we feel, as many of us have, that all our misery is caused by the actions of the alcoholic. We are eager to justify ourselves, explaining what he or she did that was so shocking, so inexcusable! Then how, we ask, could anyone think we were at fault?

Gradually we come to understand that we could have done many things more wisely. Perhaps we have criticized actions that we need not have taken to heart. We brought many troubles on ourselves, we find, by interfering. Finally we see that we have much inventorying of our own to do.

Today's Reminder

Do I habitually criticize others? I will learn to *Live and Let Live.*

Am I fearful, picturing with dread what the future will bring? I will *Let Go and Let God,* and live only for this one day.

Do I aggravate family problems with temper tantrums and uncontrolled words and actions? I will remind myself to *Think.* Am I constantly in a state of flustered confusion? I will put *First Things First.*

> "I find the Slogans a great help
> in taking a searching and fearless
> moral inventory *of myself.*"

Once I am immersed in the Al-Anon program in my search for peace of mind, I feel I am committed to the effort to understand my own drives and motives, and to correct those which are hampering me.

The search for self-understanding is a difficult, if not impossible, thing to achieve fully. But we *can* learn a lot about ourselves if we have the courage to face our real motives, without deceiving ourselves with evasions. We *can*, if we don't allow uneasy guilt feelings to obscure our good qualities, which we must recognize and build upon.

Today's Reminder

Taking my own inventory does not mean concentrating on my shortcomings until all the good is hidden from view. Recognizing the good is not an act of pride or conceit, as I may have feared. If I recognize my good qualities as God-given, I can do it with true humility while experiencing joyous satisfaction in what is pleasant, loving and generous in me.

> "I am larger, better than I thought,
>   I did not know I held so much goodness."
>
>   (*Walt Whitman*)

Sometimes it is good to examine a common-place familiar phrase, meditate on it, take it apart and explore its inner meaning.

We hear someone say: "He is standing in his own light." How clearly the picture emerges of our shadowing our own happiness by mistaken thinking. Let us stand aside so the light can shine on us and on all we do, so we can see ourselves and our circumstances with true clarity.

If we have Al-Anon, there is no need to stand in our own light and try to solve our problems in darkness. The ways and means that Al-Anon offers have lighted the way for so many thousands of despairing people that no one can question their power.

Today's Reminder

When I am faced with a problem that seems impossible to solve, when I feel trapped in a situation and can see no way out, let me ask myself whether I am *standing in my own light*. I must find the vantage point where I can most clearly see my difficulty *as it is;* then answers will come.

. . . . "and the light shall shine in dark places and make all clear as day."

One evening at a meeting there seemed to be an unusual number of complaints from members—about not having what they felt entitled to, or about the alcoholics' behavior and generally about their sorry lot in life.

One, a forthright person, spoke up:

"You know, all this sounds as though some of us were childishly expecting life to be entirely free of problems. I recall a long-ago radio comedienne whose favorite line went something like this: *'Well, you have to take the bitter with the better.'* That's pretty good Al-Anon philosophy, too, because it tells us we have to accept some unpalatable experiences along the way, never forgetting, at the same time, to keep an eye on the good things."

Today's Reminder

Am I expecting everything in life to be just the way I want it? Maybe I ought to take a good look at those expectations and see if they are realistic for my particular situation. If I'm constantly reaching for the moon, I'm going to miss a lot of pleasant things right here in my little world.

> "The Serenity Prayer is excellent medicine for discontentment."

People often marvel when they see the Al-Anon program bring about changes in the lives of those who practice it. This is its secret: that it is built on the *fundamental ethical philosophy* which has been known throughout the ages. It is stated in such widely different books as the Bible and the fables of Aesop.

To deal gently with our fellowman is suggested in St. Paul's Epistle to the Ephesians: "The fruit of the spirit is love, joy, peace, *gentleness . . ."*

The same thought appears in the fable of the wind and the sun, who challenged one another as to which could first remove the cloak of a passing traveler. As the wind blew hard and cold, the man wrapped the cloak tightly around him; then the sun shone, and its warmth made the man take off his cloak.

Today's Reminder

In Al-Anon this same thought is repeated in many ways that point out that we can do nothing by force or compulsion. I will remind myself not to be too determined in my judgments and actions.

> "Kindness is the mightiest force in
> the world. . . ."

Step One of the Twelve Steps, "admitted we were powerless," is often thought to be the most difficult of all. For some of us, though, the Second Step is just as hard, because it suggests we admit that our own behavior hasn't always been entirely sane. Here's an example:

A fairly usual habit that is irrational and self-defeating is to make big troubles out of little ones. We don't do this because we haven't enough of the big ones—oh no! It's because we're so weighed down by it all that *everything* looks black, and we fail to distinguish between what's crucial and important, and what things we could afford to ignore and forget.

Today's Reminder

Every time something happens to frustrate or annoy me, I'll stand off and ask myself: "Is this a mountain or a molehill?" I just won't waste time and nervous energy on unimportant things; I'll save them so I can cope with the big ones!

> "Some folks worry and putter,
> Push and shove,
> Hunting little molehills
> To make big mountains of."

When we try to absorb too much too quickly in Al-Anon, we may be discouraged and fail to continue with the program. But let us consider that philosophers throughout the ages spent their whole lives in contemplating such truths and, since our busy lives leave us little time for meditation and study, we would be wise to take it slowly, concentrating on one idea at a time.

Today's Reminder

I will select a single thought from one of the Twelve Steps, or a phrase from my Al-Anon reading, and try to apply it each day. This will give me a little nugget of security to which I can add other concepts as I need them. In this process we find an important application of our slogan *Easy Does It.*

I will not try to grasp the whole program at once, lest I become distracted and confused. I will remind myself that the only vital thing is to *apply* what I have learned—to make it work for me in all the happenings of my daily life.

> "If I learn nothing more in Al-Anon
> than to keep hands off what is not
> truly my business, this alone will
> lighten and brighten my life."

There are times when the "poor me" mood is upon us; we're overwhelmed by all the troubles we have to face. This is especially likely to happen when we have begun to try to change our thinking about ourselves and our relation to others. We may, at first, become too analytical and try to solve too much at once.

For this frame of mind there is an almost infallible prescription: to empty our minds of all thoughts but one: *today* and how to use it.

Today's Reminder

This day is mine. It is unique. Nobody in the world has one exactly like it. It holds the sum of all my past experience and all my future potential. It belongs to me to do with whatever I like. I can fill it with joyous moments or ruin it with fruitless worry. If painful recollections of the past come into my mind, or frightening thoughts of the future, I will put them away. They cannot spoil today for me.

> "Today is my special gift from
> God. How will I use it? The
> less I let others affect it,
> the more serene and satisfying
> it will be for me.

We make a great many decisions—small day-to-day ones that are mere choices, all the way up to big resolutions to make important changes in our lives.

Little or big, they are better when we use whatever forethought the situation requires. If they are concerned with other people, it is well to include such ingredients as love, generosity, tolerance and just plain kindness. Then we will make decisions we can live with comfortably.

If the resolution we're about to make is highly charged with anger, resentment or bitterness, it would be wise to hold back until the hysteria has subsided and we have taken time to consider all the factors calmly.

Today's Reminder

I will remember that a decision I make in a time of crisis might not be the one I would make when the crisis is past. I will not rashly take a step which I may afterward regret.

> "All our resolves and decisions are made in a mood or frame of mind which is certain to change."
>
> *(Proust)*

We get so used to hearing Al-Anon described as a *fellowship* that we sometimes forget the significance, *to each of us personally,* of that word. The Oxford English Dictionary says it is: "Participation, community of interest, sentiment and nature; the spirit of comradeship . . . especially spiritual, etc." In a fellowship, we give of ourselves and the more we give, the more we get.

If I go out of my way to help a fellow member in trouble, and try to help him or her understand a problem and deal with it spiritually, I am actually getting more than I give, for I learn from examining my own ideas and clarifying them. Many a solution to a difficulty of my own has come to me while I was helping someone else.

Today's Reminder

The good that I get from the spiritual teachings of Al-Anon will work most fully for me as I use opportunities to give it away to someone else. In this fellowship, I am but a channel for God's loving help.

> "Thou therefore which teachest
> another, teachest thou not thyself?"
> *(Ephesians)*

Al-Anon is not an organization; it has no managers or bosses. It is a fellowship of equals, held together in close union by something called "obedience to the unenforceable." This means that every group conducts Al-Anon's work according to the spiritual principles stated in our Traditions, which they accept and follow *of their own free will,* without being directed or compelled by anyone.

"But," someone may say, "the Fourth Tradition says each group should be autonomous. Doesn't that mean we can run our meetings any way we want to, use any kind of literature, and generally run things to suit ourselves?"

The answer is that the autonomy granted by the Fourth Tradition is limited to *what is good for the fellowship as a whole.* If a group departs from the ideas and procedures that make for *the greatest good for the greatest number of Al-Anon members,* it takes on its shoulders the responsibility for damaging the fellowship to which all of us look for help.

When a group faces questions or problems, the answers will be found in our Twelve Traditions. That is why it is so important for all of us to know them. The health and unity of all Al-Anon depends on the cooperation of all groups.

> "Each group should be autonomous,
> except in matters affecting another
> group or Al-Anon or AA as a whole."
> (Tradition Four)

Living with an alcoholic brings with it special problems that take many forms. If it is the
drinker's erratic behavior, social embarrassment, and other relatively minor problems, it
is but a short step, in Al-Anon, to peace of
mind for the non-alcoholic.

In others, the family may be deprived of the
very necessities of life, and face cruelty, violence, police action, loss of home and need for
public assistance.

Indignant at such sufferings, some of us in
Al-Anon may feel it right and helpful to advise
drastic action. We should always keep in
mind, however, that if the person we mean to
help makes a decision in hysteria or desperation, it is likely to be the wrong one.

Today's Reminder

Even in cases that seem hopeless to me, I will
refrain from making judgments or giving advice.
If I can persuade a desperate wife or husband to
try, for even a little while, to understand and use
the Al-Anon program, the resulting change in attitude could help to make the right solutions possible.

> "God grant that I may never urge any-
> one to take any action but the con-
> structive one of employing Al-Anon
> ideas."

What roles do we play in our relations with various people? When this topic came up in an Al-Anon meeting, a member suggested that each of us might take a closer look at our attitudes toward our families. He pointed out that here, at the Al-Anon meeting, we were often *cheerful, willing* to accept the program, *hopeful* that it would work for us.

"But do we," he asked, "always present the same pleasant face to the alcoholic and to our children? Or do we often scowl and scold, admonish and complain, so the picture we present of ourselves at home is that of boss, mentor and disapprover?"

Today's Reminder

If my attitude at home is habitually glum and critical, I will try to change this by observing what I say and do, and how my family reacts. I will not reserve my deference and respect for outsiders whom I want to please, or my pleasant expressions for those I want to impress. The people I live with are worthy of my best behavior, and will surely respond to the respect and loving kindness which, without meaning to, I may have withheld from them.

> "A merry heart doeth good like
> a medicine, but a broken spirit
> drieth the bones."
>
> (*Proverbs*)

Al-Anon, like other groupings of people with a common interest or cause, has a language of its own—certain words and phrases which describe specific ideas. We may recognize them and use them without being quite clear as to their real meaning.

Take, for instance, the phrase: "Detach from the problem, but not from the person." Some have actually imagined it means that Al-Anon advises against separation from the spouse! Others think it means shutting your mind and coldly ignoring everything that happens. Neither is true.

When we are urged to practice *detachment,* it never means *disinterest.* The latter would express only despair and hopelessness, while loving detachment gives us every hope of better days.

Today's Reminder

Of course I must be concerned with what happens to the people in my life. The purpose of emotional detachment is to keep myself from being drawn into crises of the alcoholic's making. If I do not interfere, he will be compelled to find *his own way* out of his difficulties. This is the wholesome, helpful Al-Anon kind of detachment.

> "Detachment motivated by love can
> shield us from needless pain and
> set the stage for a truly reward-
> ing relationship."

An Al-Anon member once remarked that the main source of our unhappiness is that we ourselves don't know what we want. We think we're dissatisfied with what we have, with the way we live, and the way other people act toward us. He suggested that each person dig down deep to see what we really feel would bring us contentment.

If this self-searching reveals only that we are disgruntled because we feel we deserve a better car, a bigger house or more money, we must dig still deeper for the real cause. Is it envy of others? Is it our inability to enjoy fully what we do have? Do we, in defense of our own shortcomings, look for excuses to blame others?

Today's Reminder

I can find serenity only by rooting out my discontent. I must acknowledge to myself the real reasons why I react as I do. Am I doing my share? If not, my dissatisfaction may be due to unrecognized guilt. Is it difficult for me to feel and express appreciation? I will try to develop a sense of gratitude. Do I expect others to behave according to my expectations? I will live and let live.

> "It really adds up to this: that we're
> not satisfied with ourselves, and we
> can certainly do something about that."

Once there was a Very Nice Girl whose neighbor told her about Al-Anon. The girl was very proud and only reluctantly admitted that her brother was wrecking the family by his excessive drinking. She went to a few meetings, but always hesitated when her neighbor invited her. It seemed this Very Nice Girl felt a little above the kind of people who came to talk about their drunken relatives. But the neighbor, a dedicated Al-Anon, realized that she had not yet learned the importance of Humility in coping with life's problems.

She would criticize the way people talked at meetings; commented that some of them were uneducated and used faulty grammar, and so on. Finally, after working with her patiently, the neighbor managed to convince her that the most important thing about Al-Anon was the way we help each other through love and mutual concern for each other's problems. And that the most important way to get that help was to listen to *what* is said, and not *how* it is said.

One day the neighbor, who read the Bible each morning and evening, came across a paragraph that she thought would be helpful— and it was! This is what it said:

"There are, it may be, so many kinds of voices in the world, and none of them is without significance." This verse, from the 14th Chapter of 1st Corinthians, verse 10, made it clear to the girl that she would find answers from *uncritical* listening. And she did!

Heard at an Al-Anon meeting: "I am willing to admit that the Al-Anon program, as a personal discipline, can do a lot for anyone who uses it. But I can't believe that we need the help of what you call a Higher Power, or God."

Even for those of us who believe only what we can see and touch, there is help in Al-Anon. Gradually, as we experience the miraculous results of using the Twelve Steps (even if only those which make no reference to the spiritual!) we are led to believe in a Power greater than ourselves. We receive, through spiritual enlightenment, the gift of faith. Finally we come to realize that the good changes in our lives could not have come about without God's guidance.

Today's Reminder

If we admit the reality of our problems, and we can realistically appraise the experience of working them out, we have the most rational of reasons for believing in a Higher Power. We see, then, that we can use a Source of help which is beyond our human understanding.

> "Why should we try to move mountains
> with our own strength alone
> when faith, 'even as a grain of
> mustard seed', can help us achieve
> what seemed impossible?"

"Sought through prayer and meditation *to improve our conscious contact with God . . ."* says Step Eleven. This gives me the assurance that my conscious contact with Him depends entirely on me, on *my* desire for it. This great power is mine, constantly near and available for me to use.

Today's Reminder

I will remind myself every day how much depends on my being aware of God's influence in my life. I will accept His help in everything I do. Without such surrender to a superior wisdom, my life would be at the mercy of forces I cannot control.

Meditation will bring me closer to God and to the divine qualities in my fellowmen who are also His children. Prayer will turn my thoughts away from my problems. As I meditate and pray, I am letting go of them and learning that their solution does not depend on me alone.

> "God is present in all His creatures,
> but all are not equally
> aware of His presence."

If I could make a clear distinction between *self-love* and love of self, it would be a giant step forward in changing my attitude toward the alcoholic. Self-love is the source of hostility and arrogance, the big ego around which everything must revolve. It makes me unable to see any point of view but my own. It is the mark of a mind which is closed to real feeling for others.

Love of self, on the other hand, carries out the Commandment: "Thou shalt love thy neighbor as *thyself*." We can love others, and help them, only when we are at peace with ourselves. When we appreciate our own dignity and value as human beings, we are better able to have compassion for others.

Today's Reminder

Self-love often wears a mask of false humility behind which we exaggerate our own importance, and justify the wrongs we do to others. True humility comes from love of self, which is the realization of ourselves as we really are.

> "Resolve to be thyself and know
> that he who finds himself loses
> his misery."
>
> (*Matthew Arnold*)

There are those who come to Al-Anon weighed down by an unbearable problem. They expect that it can be solved by human means alone, but they soon learn that the help they get is provided by human beings *acting as channels for the love and wisdom of a Higher Power*.

Perhaps they have never had the security and comfort of a living faith; often they have lost what faith they once had because of misfortunes that have befallen them. They may feel that God has been cruel and unfair, that He is not concerned with them and their burdens. Some, in utter despair, actually think they are not worthy of God's care.

Today's Reminder

Divine help is *always near and available* to me —if I am willing to accept it. Active consciousness, at all times, of "not my will, but Thine, be done" will work out every difficulty.

> "Short arm needs man to reach to Heaven,
> So ready is Heaven to stoop to him."
> (Francis Thompson: *Grace of the Way*)

Here is another Al-Anon prescription for that frantic state of tension we call being "tied in knots."

Just for the moment, empty your mind of all thought. Then admit to it one single idea, and concentrate on it for a whole minute. Let it be a simple thing you can make a picture of in your mind—a rose of a specific color, an empty bowl you imagine yourself filling with bright fruit; a tiny sliver of a new moon. Think of nothing else but that one thing and don't let anything else intrude. The minute will seem like an hour, but at the end of this concentrated thought, the tension and confusion will have drained away, and you'll be better able to cope with the present problem.

Today's Reminder

Troubles grow bigger as we spend more and more time thinking about them. I will interrupt such thoughts with a meditation whenever their weight is too much for me. It will calm my thinking and put my difficulty into proper focus.

> "Meditation is the spiritual way
> to turn my thoughts away from what-
> ever is troubling me. It is a
> lift, a refreshment."

Familiar phrases often fall on deaf ears; even when we listen thoughtfully, we may not analyze their deeper meaning because we're so used to hearing them.

One evening a new member, explaining her problem, several times used the phrase: "It just makes me sick." The idea she meant to convey was "unbearable" or "frustrating." But another member, who took it literally, said:

"I was impressed with Jane's saying that certain occurrences *make her sick*. I've noticed that when *I* react too emotionally to a situation, even an unjustified verbal attack, it really can make me sick, with actual physical symptoms. Al-Anon has taught me to keep my own well-being in mind; I try not to let myself feel involved when the storm clouds of tension and temper appear. This is healthy thinking—the Al-Anon way."

Today's Reminder

I will close my mind to what I hear and see when it tempts me to quarrel or resent. I will receive anger with gentleness to guard my peace of mind.

> "It takes time to transform good
> resolutions into good habits,
> but it's worth the effort."

"Listen and learn" is the Al-Anon prescription. We could all make good progress if only we would cultivate the knack of listening—*uncritically*—to everything we hear at a meeting, or from an Al-Anon friend.

It sometimes happens that the words of those who are unschooled, or those who are negative and confused, can bring us a sudden gem of thought that will help us. If we're concentrating on dark thoughts about our own problems, we could be missing something that might help us overcome them. If we are contemptuous of some downtrodden, unkempt mortal, using ungrammatical language, our attitude may deprive us of an unexpectedly helpful idea.

Today's Reminder

An old hymn says: "I will listen for Thy voice, lest my footsteps stray", which may remind us that His voice speaks to us even through the least of His children.

The essential quality of good listening is humility. A holier-than-thou attitude can block out much that we need for our guidance.

"It is the privilege of wisdom to listen."

(O. W. Holmes)

Once upon a time a new member came to Al-Anon, full of trouble and confusion. She was a willing learner, studied the Steps and tried to use them. The Miraculous Change (the one we're all searching for) came to her quite soon, and everyone marveled. One evening she was asked to speak:

"I was eager to *get* the program, so I read all the Steps at once before starting to work on them one by one. One word in the Eleventh Step stopped me: *meditation.* Each morning I set aside ten minutes, and tried to keep my mind on *one subject,* thinking of all its elements and qualities. At first I concentrated on the idea of this day to which I had awakened. I'd say 'Here is a day full of hours and minutes in which nothing has yet happened. I've made no mistakes, suffered no trouble.' Just then my wilful mind switched over to the happenings of the days just past and I found myself reliving all the horrors. 'Stop!' I said: 'You've lost track of your meditation!' and back I went to the contemplation of this one single unmarred day. Again my mind took off in another direction: dread of tomorrow. And again I brought it back to the subject of *today* and its unlimited possibilities.

"Gradually it grew easier to make myself concentrate on one idea, without straying into thoughts of resentment and fear. I am sure these meditations are giving me a sense of reality about my life. I use it on the Steps, on the Serenity Prayer, and on any helpful spiritual idea. It really works."

It seems strange, when I think of it, that God is most vivid to my consciousness when I am in the depths of despair, and all I can say to Him is: "God help me!"

And He does help us when we turn to Him in our great need, for "man's extremity is God's opportunity." An equally imperative reason for prayer is to acknowledge our gratitude. Gratitude is in itself a wholesome and healing force and it becomes all the more real when we make it a regular part of our prayers.

Those of us who lived so long with alcoholism, and can now enjoy the recovery of a loved one from this sickness, have good reasons for prayers of gratitude.

Today's Reminder

I will keep myself aware of the many blessings that come to me each day and remember to be thankful for them.

> "You pray in your distress and in your need; would that you might pray also in the fullness of your joy."
> (Kahlil Gibran: *The Prophet*)

One way Al-Anon is a big help is that it reminds me of truths I tend to forget. For example, I hear again and again at meetings, and read in the Al-Anon literature: *Alcoholism is a disease—the alcoholic is a sick human being—we do not punish people for being sick.*

I may give ample lip service to this idea, but when it comes to real acceptance, my instinctive attitude toward the alcoholic is often hostile, as though he were an enemy, wilfully bent on destroying me. I need Al-Anon's constant reminders that such feelings hinder both my spiritual progress and improvement in the family situation. I must rid myself of the poison of resentment, indignation at a person I am not capable of judging fairly, and useless pity for myself.

Today's Reminder

If I am suffering from bitterness against the alcoholic, I will cling to the thought that my growth and serenity depend on overcoming my animosity. Unless I free myself from it, I may carry it over into my relations with other people, even those who, in Al-Anon, are trying to help me.

> "It is not men's acts which disturb us—
> but our reaction to them. Take these
> away, and anger goes. No wrong act of
> another can bring shame on you."
>
> (*Marcus Aurelius*)

"It's all very well to tell us to detach our minds from the problems we're living with, but how do you do it?" asks an Al-Anon member. "It isn't easy when we're embroiled in all kinds of trouble day after day, with one decision after another to make, and only a confused mind to make them with!"

There must be some small bit of time during the day when we can lift our thoughts out of the swamp of confusion, if only to express a few words and think of their meaning: *Let go and Let God; Live and let live; Easy does it.*

Today's Reminder

I know that constant dwelling on my troubles lessens my ability to see them clearly and make wise decisions. I will not complicate the present by reviewing the past; nor will I dread what may happen tomorrow. One way to make detachment easier is to eliminate the past and future from my thoughts.

> "He who frees himself of hampering regrets for the past and worry about what lies ahead finds himself able to deal with the present."

If I have made myself a part of an Al Anon group to get help, wouldn't I be defeating myself if I allowed what we call personality clashes to interfere with my getting the full benefit of the program?

Individuals tend to be more or less dominant; sometimes the most competent and helpful assert themselves over-strongly and so engender hostility in others. Sometimes there just isn't a personal rapport between two people.

I want to keep in mind always that *my help depends on the unity of the group.* I will not allow myself to resent what anyone does; I will accept the fact that they mean to be helpful, no matter what they may say or do.

Today's Reminder

I will make a conscious effort to look for the good in every person in my group. I will not criticize anyone on a personal basis. If there are disagreements on principles, they can always be resolved by consulting the Twelve Steps and Twelve Traditions.

> "We penalize ourselves when we allow
> disapproval of another person to
> endanger the unity of the group.
> Anything that damages the group
> interferes with its ability to
> function for the good of each
> person in it."

As a member of Al-Anon, I am part of a group which is part of a fellowship of thousands of such groups, encircling the world. One cannot even imagine the many kinds of people who join Al-Anon for the same purpose as I did: to learn a better way of life despite the difficulties of living with an alcoholic. Their social units and customs are different from mine—the spirit that motivates us is the same. This holds us together as one united fellowship wherever in the world we may be.

Today's Reminder

In one sense, I have an obligation to members of every group, not only my own. That duty is to observe and preserve Al-Anon's principles and Traditions. The principles, for the individual, are stated in the Twelve Steps. The Traditions, also Twelve, are for group guidance. It is important to all Al-Anon, and to me personally, to know both the Steps and the Traditions and protect them from distortion and dilution. I will read them and try to apply them in both personal and group matters.

> Tradition One: "Our common welfare should come first; personal progress for the greatest number depends upon unity."

Told by a member at an Al-Anon meeting:

"During my first year in Al-Anon, I concentrated on changing my attitude toward the alcoholic. I learned to sidestep quarrels; I controlled my impulse to complain and scold. I worked hard on getting rid of my resentments. As our relationship improved, and he was in AA, I had less reason to feel sorry for myself. I *thought* I was working the program.

"But all was not well in the home. There was a constant undercurrent of minor irritations. I had gone overboard trying to distract my mind from concentrating on the alcoholic problem. Golf, bowling, bridge, reading and socializing didn't leave me enough time and thought my children; my house was never in order; meals were a bother. I wasn't doing my job!"

Today's Reminder

"Suddenly I awoke to the fact that Al-Anon asks a lot more of us than just to cope with the problem of alcoholism. We need to apply it to all departments of living—*and in the order of their importance.*"

> "I pray to remember to attend to
> first things first."

"Our group," explains a member, "concentrates on the Twelve Steps. We rarely discuss the Traditions, because we feel that *personal* guidance for individuals is more helpful to us than pointers relating to the functioning of the group."

This is warped thinking, for the fact is that the Traditions are essential to the survival and proper functioning of the group *through which each individual gets the desired help.*

The Traditions tell us, for example, that the officers of a group are its leaders. Guided by the light of Tradition Two, they will not dominate or direct, as sometimes happens when a strong-willed, opinionated member insists on holding office term after term, and makes decisions for the group.

Today's Reminder

"Our leaders are but trusted servants—they do not govern." They serve, but do not control. Al-Anon is a fellowship of equals, and each member should welcome an opportunity to serve. Who, then, provides the authority under which the groups function? Tradition Two says: "For our group purpose there is but one authority, a loving God as He may express Himself in our group conscience."

> "Everyone should realize that our groping
> and reaching toward peace of mind depend.
> very much on our attitudes within the
> Al-Anon group."

Someone persuaded Mr. J. to attend an Al-Anon meeting. His wife had finally joined AA and was devoting herself to sobriety—and to developing herself as a person through the spiritual elements in the AA program.

Mr. J. frankly didn't like it. He and his wife had entertained a great deal, at cocktail parties and such, and her sobriety interfered with these activities. To him it was perfectly ridiculous that anyone of their social standing should admit to being enslaved by alcohol. Even after four or five Al-Anon meetings, he still couldn't understand why his wife found it necessary to continue with AA now that she was sober, or that Al-Anon had anything for him.

Today's Reminder

When I consider how people limit themselves by keeping closed minds, I learn that pride often makes recovery difficult both from alcoholism and from the emotional sickness of living with an alcoholic. I see how necessary it is to accept changes in my patterns of living—if I really hope for a serene and orderly existence.

> "Some people don't know how badly
> they need a new way of life until
> disaster overtakes them."

It is strange to think that many groups are hardly aware of the Twelve Traditions, and their importance in keeping an Al-Anon group strong and united. The Traditions guard us from the destructive effects of dominance by individual members. They make us all equal, so we can work together in harmony to achieve our spiritual growth and understanding.

When each member of the group is familiar with the Traditions and helps to make them work in the group, we are safe from many of the hazards that beset people who come together for a particular purpose.

In Al-Anon, *conflicting* views become merely *differing* views, so our problems can be solved with tolerant understanding and mutual respect.

When problems arise, we refer to Chapter 10 of *Living With An Alcoholic,* where we find explanations and solutions arrived at through the Twelve Traditions.

Today's Reminder

I will make it my business to familiarize myself with the Twelve Traditions of Al-Anon, so I can do my part toward promoting growth for the group and each member in it.

> "Our common welfare should come first; personal progress for the greatest number depends upon unity.
>
> (Tradition One)

Just for today I will not be afraid of anything. If my mind is clouded with nameless dreads, I will track them down and expose their unreality. I will remind myself that God is in charge of me and mine and that I have only to *accept* His protection and guidance. What happened yesterday need not trouble me today.

This is a brand new shining day and I have it in my power to make it a good one just by the way I think about it and what I do with it.

Today's Reminder

If I live just this one day at a time, I will not so readily entertain fears of what *might* happen tomorrow. If I am concentrating on today's activities, there will be no room in my mind for fretting and worrying. I will fill every minute of this day with something good—seen, heard, accomplished. Then when the day is ended, I can look back on it with satisfaction and serenity.

> "I recall the words of an old
> ditty that said: 'never trouble
> trouble till trouble troubles you.' "

A fairly usual idea in some Al-Anon groups is that we attend meetings only to hear other people's tragic stories—blow-by-blow descriptions that we can perhaps identify with. This is one—*but only one*—of Al-Anon's functions. But when the stories are a continual rehash of the alcoholic's misdeeds, nobody learns anything except that we all go through pretty much the same experiences. Where is the growth in that?

If I want to determine how much help a meeting can give, I should ask myself: "How many of the people here tonight have learned something new about applying Al-Anon principles? How many have given me a constructive idea to take away with me and use?" That is the only measure of a truly valuable meeting.

Today's Reminder

What I say at an Al-Anon meeting should not be a recital of the details of someone else's faults and actions. I have come to get knowledge of how to deal with my frustrations and difficulties, and to impart what I have learned in Al-Anon to the others. Personal problems can be discussed with my sponsor or another Al-Anon friend.

> "A truly valuable Al-Anon meeting is
> one in which we concentrate on
> principles, and do not discuss
> personalities."

It sometimes happens that an Al-Anon member, deeply dedicated to some particular cause or religious organization, tries to persuade the group to share her enthusiasm and take part in it.

As worthy as a project might be, it is well to remember that Al-Anon's primary purpose is to learn how to achieve serenity for ourselves while living with the problem of alcoholism. Our Third Tradition points out that it would be unwise for us to take on, as a group, any interests not related to our program. For reasons of our own well-being and progress, we do not involve ourselves with other causes or organizations, although individuals are certainly free to do so if they wish.

Today's Reminder

Tradition Three states in unmistakable terms Al-Anon's single-minded dedication to one common denominator: "The relatives of alcoholics, when gathered together for mutual aid, may call themselves an Al-Anon group, provided that, as a group, they have no other affiliation."

> ". . . through our Traditions we guard
> against distortion and dilution
> of the Al-Anon idea."

People in trouble look for help and often ask for it in the shape of advice from the more seasoned members who are all so willing to help them.

"My husband comes home drunk and turns on the TV and keeps us awake; what shall I do?" "He was arrested for fighting; what shall I do?" "I'm sick of sitting at home all the time; he never takes me anywhere; what shall I do?"

The more experienced member realizes that *we don't tell anybody what to do.* People only accept and use the advice they're ready for. Helping the newcomer apply Al-Anon principles to all problems is a vital part of the learning process through which all of us grow. Then we will know how to make the decisions that are best for us, and have the courage to see them through.

Today's Reminder

When I am asked for advice, I know only what I would do if I were faced with the same problem, and not what would be right for another. Good advice in Al-Anon takes the form of gentle guidance into Al-Anon principles, so people can find the right answers for themselves.

"I cannot solve anyone else's problem. I can, however, show how problem-solving is done by using the Al-Anon program."

A man whose wife is an alcoholic often hesi-
tates to seek help in Al-Anon because it seems
like a confession of failure on his part. He may
be reluctant to let go of the martyrdom of
carrying the entire responsibility for the family; perhaps he derives an inner satisfaction
from the dependency of the alcoholic, whom
he considers weak and helpless.

In the Al-Anon program he can learn to
make himself comfortable by not accepting his
wife's responsibilities. He will in time discover
his own motivations and change his attitudes.
And he will do nothing toward controlling his
wife's sickness, for the First Step assures him
that he cannot.

Today's Reminder

When a man sees the logic and promise in the
Al-Anon idea, he will accept the necessity of re-
leasing his wife from his solicitous domination.
He will realize that she will seek sobriety only
when he allows her to face her problem. His search
for help is thus not a confession of failure, but
proof of his strength to reach out for a new life for
his family.

> "If that thou hast the gift of strength,
>   then know thy part is to uplift the
>   trodden low."
>   (George Meredith: *The Burden of Strength*)

We hear in Al-Anon that no situation is hopeless. At first we find this hard to believe. Hope and despair are *human emotional attitudes;* it is *we* who are hopeless, and not the condition of our lives. In a desperate situation, we give up hope because we are unable, as yet, to believe in the possibility of a change for the better.

Today's Reminder

If I have been relying on my judgment alone, and have tried to correct what is wrong by using the wrong tools, I have reason for despair. I will learn, in Al-Anon, to recognize my errors, to see the roadblocks of self-will and self-righteousness I have been putting in my way. Then I will no longer insist that a thing is impossible because *I* have been unable to accomplish it. Others have, and many of them had far greater problems than mine. Once I use the Al-Anon program and let myself be guided by God's will instead of my own, my distorted outlook will be replaced by order and peace of mind.

> ". . . if thou canst believe; all things are possible to him that believeth."
>
> *(Mark)*

In one of the Al-Anon leaflets the following hard-to-believe statement is made: *"A drinking problem in the home can often be more easily recognized by the wife's behavior than by that of the drinker."*

Isn't this an inevitable consequence of our turbulent emotions, our despair and uncertainty? Isn't it proved by our futile efforts to outwit the alcoholic, to compel him to stop drinking and meet his responsibilities? This self-imposed struggle to control the uncontrollable is certainly not rational!

Once we experience the effects of applying the Al-Anon program, and observe the miraculous changes that take place in the attitudes of our Al-Anon friends, we can look back thankfully that we, too, are improving our relationships.

Today's Reminder

As I see the progress I have made, it becomes clear to me that many of my earlier habitual reactions needed to be transformed into normal mature behavior. The only possible way to improve the conditions of one's life is to improve one's emotional condition.

> "Most of the things I did, in anger
> and frustration, only made matters
> worse. Now I am learning to let go."

One of the ways in which we help ourselves to serenity and an orderly life is through Twelfth Step work, so-called because it is the final one of the Twelve Steps by which we live in Al-Anon.

It means to be always ready to help another person in trouble—someone new who may not yet have heard that Al-Anon can help when there is alcoholism in a family. This "carrying the message" requires constant awareness of a possible need: perhaps a neighbor or someone we meet casually who indicates that he or she is living with such a problem.

Today's Reminder

I will tactfully offer help to anyone who needs to learn how to live with all the many difficulties which alcoholism can create or aggravate. My first suggestion should be that there is always hope, and that a new way of life can be found in Al-Anon, in the company of others who share the same problem.

> "I will be always ready to carry the message to others. The need is all around me if I keep myself alert enough to recognize it. In helping others, I also help myself."

Throughout this month, which brings us to the closing of another year, I will review the happenings of my life as though I were standing just a little way off trying to see myself as another person.

Have I made progress in my effort to correct my faulty attitudes? Have I let discouragement plunge me back into my old habit patterns? When something I did had consequences that made life difficult for me, did I try to blame someone else?

How has Al-Anon helped me to realize some of my potential as a person?

Today's Reminder

As I look back over this year, I will consider calmly my actions and attitudes, just as though I were evaluating the progress of someone else. I will not make it an occasion for guilt and regret. I will blame no one else for anything that happened, for I have learned in Al-Anon that I am not a judge of others. This day, and the days to come, will be filled with opportunities to make more of myself.

> "The purpose of my inventory is to get a clear picture of where I now stand, to recognize shortcomings that still need to be corrected, and not to use any self-deceiving means of justifying them.

When we're at a meeting, the Al-Anon ideas seem so clear to us that we never doubt we can apply them to our daily living. But alas, the old thinking patterns take over and we have what corresponds in AA to a "slip" or a relapse. This is no reason to be discouraged.

If I look back on my pre-Al-Anon attitude, I can see how much I have learned, and how much of it I *do* remember to use in dealing with my everyday problems. Perfect mastery is too much for me to expect of myself; I will be patient.

Today's Reminder

If it isn't easy for me to "see myself as others see me" and recognize how much progress I have made, all I need to do is to observe the improvement in the others in my group. Even some that appeared to have "hopeless" problems make great strides in learning to detach from many of the harrowing episodes in the alcoholism. They recognize that *their* thinking and *their* actions were not always sane either. They use the Al-Anon program to restore themselves to a reasonable and serene frame of mind.

> "Al-Anon doesn't produce miracles
> overnight, but when we look back,
> we realize that a miracle is in
> the process of taking place."

There are questions—and many of us ask them—that lead us straight down the dead-end street of frustration: "Why can't he . . . ?" —"What is he up to?" —"Why can't I make him see . . . ?"

They're simple, but they say a lot. They reveal our conviction that we're in control—that *we* know what ought to be done—that our wisdom is greater than someone else's. They lead to frustration because we're *not* in control—of anyone or anything but ourselves.

In his book, *The Sign of Jonas*, the noted writer Thomas Merton says:

"Stop asking yourself questions that have no meaning. Or if they have, you'll find out when you need to—find out both the questions and the answers."

Today's Reminder

I will rather ask myself *"What prompts me to do or say things that cause trouble?"*—*"Why do I concentrate on someone else's shortcomings instead of my own?"* To such questions I can find the answers—if I dig deeply and honestly enough.

"Speculating on other people's attitudes and motives is a waste of time and effort To search out the reasons for my own is a voyage of discovery!"

Some of us come to Al-Anon to find out *why* the alcoholic drinks. We're afraid it's because "he doesn't love me any more" or because something we have done or are doing is upsetting him and making him drink.

We are much relieved to learn that alcoholism is an illness. It is also helpful, however, to know that the very things we have been doing may have hindered recovery from this illness.

With the best of intentions, we have been trying to cure it by treating it as deliberately wilful and wicked. We are told that anything we do to humiliate and blame the alcoholic only increases his guilt or reinforces his claim that we are at fault. This teaches us the immense value of a hands-off policy. It is hard to come by, but it works wonders!

Today's Reminder

I will not waste thought on exploring the reasons why the alcoholic drinks. Al-Anon answers that I can cope with my problems effectively by *changing my thinking about them*, correcting my own mistaken attitudes, and allowing the alcoholic to take care of his own problem.

> "I ask God to help keep me on the course that will change my life for the better."

Life with the Al-Anon program, to which we turn when we are deep in trouble, may ultimately confront us with a special challenge.

At first we may come as doubters: "How can my terrible problem be solved by joining a group?" Then come the revelations. We learn how to live and find serenity in the midst of alcoholic turmoil. We see ourselves growing, understanding, helping.

But once the major problem is eliminated by the alcoholic's joining AA, we may feel we're old-timers at this Al-Anon business; we think we "have it made." We skip meetings; have no time to comfort troubled newcomers, forget about reading Al-Anon books.

Then comes the challenge of continued problems, and we realize how much we still need Al-Anon to keep ourselves able to meet them.

Today's Reminder

I don't resort to Al-Anon only to learn to live with the active drinking problem. It is my way of life, an increasingly rich and rewarding life, as I learn to use the program in depth.

"AA brings the drinker to sobriety in
order to fit him to absorb the deeper
meanings of the program. Al-Anon
changes our thinking for the same purpose."

More than two thousand years ago an ancient philosopher wrote some words of wisdom whose central ideas seem strangely modern to us who study the Twelve Steps. They concern the errors we humans, since the beginning of time, seem to fall into:

A man is not complete who believes that his advancement depends on crushing others—

Or who worries about matters that cannot be altered—

Or who insists that a thing is impossible because he has not been able to do it.

That man is short of wisdom who cannot put aside his ordinary routine in order to refresh his mind with rest, change and meditation.

He needs much help who thinks he can compel others to do what seems right to him.

Today's Reminder

Words of wisdom inspire us, but they have value only if we can take them into our hearts and use them in our daily lives.

"The basic truths which are placed
before me in Al-Anon have immeasurable
power to help me."

These words, long thought to have been dated 1692 and found, so the legend goes, in a Baltimore churchyard, were actually the inspiring work of a modern Boston poet named Max Ehrmann, and dated 1927. Its apt title: *Desiderata* *

"Go placidly amid the noise and haste, and remember what peace there may be in silence. As far as possible without surrender, be on good terms with all persons. Speak your truth quietly and clearly; listen to others, even the dull and ignorant; they, too, have their story."

Today's Reminder

Like our Serenity Prayer, repeating these phrases each morning could establish our mood for that day—and make the day a good one. It could serve as a reminder that we must watch the quality of our own deportment, and as we learn in Al-Anon, everything depends on that!

"I will not let my inner peace be disturbed by the confusions around me. I will be gentle and tolerant, while maintaining my right to my individuality. I will listen and appreciate, and not judge the source of what I hear."

* This corrects a regrettable error made in earlier editions of this book.

It's a sad day for an Al-Anon group when its members settle down into old-timer status and the meetings are mere get-togethers for a bit of chatting and gossip.

Gone is the vitality and hope that inspired the group in the early days—gone the eager exchange of experience, strength and hope, the challenge to apply the program to every department of life. And gone is the hand of friendship that reached out to troubled people and drew them into the fold to learn about the Steps to serenity, confidence, renewed faith—all accomplished through our helping and caring.

Today's Reminder

I will not forget that the possibilities of this vast spiritual program are still limitless for me. I still have much to learn in it. Let me remember, too, that an Al-Anon group is a vital feature of any community; there are so many to whom it could bring hope! I will try to find them, through churches, doctors, courts and counselors—and share Al-Anon with them.

"Each day is a new adventure in Al-Anon, pointing the way to an ever-better way to live."

It is heartening to know that Al-Anon members can be a world-wide inspiration to each other; thoughts and prayers fly across space to sustain and strengthen us all. These wise words come from the Al-Anon groups of France:

"We have all had the feeling of being chained to a heavy weight that we were trying to drag this way and that, while all the time it was dragging *us* until we completely lost our bearings.

"Now there is another chain for us; the one that unites us in Al-Anon. Each of us is a link, neither more nor less important than all the rest. It is a chain to which we can attach ourselves whenever we need it."

Today's Reminder

What a relief to be able to detach ourselves from the chain that bound us to the weight of alcoholism—to know we need *not* be helplessly controlled by it. We are freed by knowing we cannot exert the slightest influence on it. How light and pleasant it is to be a link in that other chain that binds us together in Al-Anon, and to discover how to correct the attitudes that kept us chained to our anxieties.

> "He that handleth a matter
> wisely shall find good."

(*Proverbs*)

My life is a series of unfoldings—incidents and occasions, agreeable or distressing. Each day is full of them, hour by hour, and this makes it difficult for me to take a detached view of all that is happening. I'm too close.

If these occurrences were like so many pieces of merchandise—groceries or dry goods —I would see them clearly, good and bad. Looking at the incidents of my life in this way, I might be astonished to discover that the good far outweigh the bad. And yet I concentrate so heavily on my trials and burdens that I hardly give a thought to relishing the pleasant and satisfying things that happen each day.

This *noticing* is an acute awareness of our surroundings and what takes place in them. It can be cultivated, like watching a play or film.

Today's Reminder

If I learn to see everything with a fresh eye, I will find I have many reasons for contentment and gratitude. When I find myself being bogged down with negative thoughts, I will deliberately turn away from them.

> "Let me observe, with new interest, even the commonplace things that happen in each new day."

It is often emphasized in Al-Anon writings and in talk at meetings that ours is not a religious program, but a spiritual one. The central truth of all worship, creed, church or dogma is that *God is the essence of our being,* and this is the *spiritual* idea of Al-Anon.

If we stop going to church we may think we are disposing of a God who has disappointed us. We may see Him as a punisher who has sought us out with unmerited pain and suffering. However we regard Him, or even if we do not recognize Him at all, He is always there, within us, within every thing and every person in the universe, constantly available for our help if we are willing to accept. How well we use the consciousness of God in our daily lives depends not on Him, but on us.

Today's Reminder

I have observed that those who make the best progress in the Al-Anon program are those who readily accept the help of a Higher Power. Once they can do that, it is easier for them to Let go and Let God, and their problems resolve themselves in a way that passes human understanding.

> "Lord, thou has been our dwelling
> place in all generations."
>
> (*Psalms*)

How great is the human need for a scape-goat, someone or something to blame for our disappointments. "If she hadn't done that, this wouldn't have happened."—"Why couldn't he have done what I expected?"—"It's all her fault!"

I must realize that every time I feel someone has offended or injured me, at least part of my unhappiness is due to the way I reacted. Actually I am not so vulnerable to being hurt, by circumstances or the actions of other people, as I think I am. Much that happens to me, good or bad, is self-created.

Today's Reminder

If I am convinced that I am to a large extent "the captain of my soul" I can more readily accept the fact that I have the power to ward off misfortunes, disappointments and other troubles. Blaming others for what happens to me would keep me at a spiritual standstill.

> "Nothing can work damage to me
> except myself; the harm that I
> sustain I carry about with me
> and never am a real sufferer
> except by my own fault."
> (Ralph Waldo Emerson, *quoting St. Bernard, in the Essay on Compensation*)

Let us imagine a person coming into Al-Anon, despairing and confused by the havoc wrought by alcoholism. She finds warm friendship from people willing to share their time, thought and experience with her. She gets Al-Anon literature and studies it. Finally she learns how to achieve serenity in the midst of turmoil. Her life gets better. Much has been done for her in Al-Anon.

Has she an obligation to the group, to the fellowship, and to the newcomers who need her help? The obvious answer is *Yes.* The real answer is *No.* She is not *required* to pay back in kind for any of the benefits she has had. Her only obligation is to *herself;* she owes herself the continued growth she will derive from *giving to others what she has received.*

Today's Reminder

Sharing enriches my life. Even when I serve the group as an officer, or do the small chores at meetings, it is wholesome therapy. I have a need to comfort and guide the troubled newcomer, because it gives me new insight into my own still faulty attitudes.

> "At no point in my life will I achieve perfection; there will never be a time when I will not need the joy and satisfaction of helping others."

"Sponsorship—What It's All About" is the title of a booklet available to any member. This is a new thought to many of us. We may doubt that we're strong enough in the program—we may think we "haven't time to take on somebody else's troubles." Being a sponsor is a great adventure. It is more than that—it is a great education in human relations and in spiritual growth.

Once we start, we're amazed to find how much we have absorbed of the Al-Anon program. And from this personal interchange and sharing, the sponsor often gains even more than the sponsored!

Today's Reminder

It is not only the newcomer who benefits from having one particular person to look to for guidance—even the old-timer in the program may find that another member, with different and perhaps better insights, can be of immense help. As one member put it: ". .answers came not from books, but from mutual caring and thinking out loud with someone you felt comfortable with."

"I would strongly recommend sponsorship to anyone in Al-Anon. It opens a whole new area of mind and heart; it's a big job and you have to grow in it."

I am learning to recognize in myself any immoderate emotional reactions to things that happen, or to something that is said to me. If I notice that I still squirm and agonize over past mistakes and disappointments, I will observe that and correct it. Likewise I will guard against thoughts of dread of what may happen in the future. How can I know what's going to be?

This awareness comes through the study of the Al-Anon program. It shows me how to overcome these handicaps by taking care of just one little day at a time.

This one day I can easily cope with, if I have not frittered away my energies on destructive emotions, and if I do not provoke antagonism by criticisms, complaints and reproaches.

Today's Reminder

When anything happens to disturb me on this one day, I will ask myself: "Is it *my* problem?"—"Does it really matter so much?"—"Is it important?"

> "Today I will observe how I react,
>   and what I am tempted to say or do."

There are the super-optimists who imagine that Al-Anon has a magic formula for curing all life's ills. A weekly hour for a meeting, they think, and all will be well.

A situation in which the lives and sanity of an entire family are at stake is not so easily solved, but the super-optimist resolutely clings to the illusion that Al-Anon can fix everything. It "fixes" nothing; that is up to us. Not in the once-a-week meeting alone, but with plenty of in-between reading, constant recall of the principles and *constant use*. Al-Anon does have the formula, but it is *we* who must use it.

Today's Reminder

Changing our whole way of thinking is a monumental task, not to be taken lightly. But many thousands of members can testify that it's the most rewarding and self-serving activity ever devised for curing sick family relationships!

> " 'Listen, read, think, use' says
> Al-Anon to those who really want a
> better way of living."

The husband of an alcoholic from an Al-Anon group in France, writes to the World Service Office: "I recall our blackboard at school, the writing was often hard to read because the board had been wiped with a cloth that was loaded with chalk-dust. Then we would wipe it with a wet sponge and the board would be clean and black, so we could read clearly what was written on it.

"Is it not the same with the anxieties that trouble me? If I wish to erase them from my mind, I must not use a cloth full of dusty thoughts, but 'pass the sponge over it' so that no trace of what was written before can jumble up the fresh inspiration—the ideas I want to see and live with."

Today's Reminder

From every corner of the world people in Al-Anon reach out to each other with helpful thoughts. How vividly this young Parisian husband shows us the need to erase our useless anxieties from our minds and hearts!

"I pray that I may start each new day
with a clean blackboard and write upon
it only what is good for me."

Thoughts to take to an Al-Anon meeting:

I will make sure that what I say will be helpful to someone, and not merely use the meeting as an audience for my troubles.

I will listen to everything that is said so I will have some constructive ideas to take home with me and use.

I will not yield to my compulsion to go on talking after I have made my point—and what I say will have a direct relevance to the subject of the meeting.

If someone asks for advice, I will give it only in terms of Al-Anon principles, and not suggest action to be taken.

Today's Reminder

The Al-Anon meeting is essentially group therapy from which each person should derive maximum benefit. If I have a personal problem to discuss, I will talk about it to my sponsor before or after the meeting, or by telephone between meetings.

> "I will not waste a single minute
> of that one hour of the week when
> we can be together to share
> experience, strength and hope."

There are 168 hours in each week. Those who come to Al-Anon for help have many of those hours filled with disturbing and even painful experience: uncertainty, unfilled needs and even violence. There are ways to overcome much of this distress, and Al-Anon offers us one way.

Isn't it worth one little hour out of 168 to come to an Al-Anon meeting? Isn't it worth ten minutes a day for reading the Al-Anon books that tell us what we can do to help ourselves, and perhaps half an hour to give a lift to another person in trouble?

Today's Reminder

It takes so little time out of the week to learn how Al-Anon applies to me and my chaotic life that the changes I can bring about seem like miracles. Living the Al-Anon way is an *every* day program, and the more thought I give to it, the greater my rewards will be—in contentment, fulfillment and constant spiritual growth.

> "Every minute I use in thinking and
> using the Al-Anon program makes all
> the hours of my week more livable."

Al-Anon gives me a priceless opportunity to do something for others. But let me not overlook the fact that helping someone else *gives me more than I give.* I have the satisfaction of lightening another's burdens. I can clear up misconceptions about the program that will help my friend make greater strides in setting her life in order. This in itself would be ample reward for me. But I also have the self-helping experience of clarifying my thoughts and seeing my own problems in a new light.

Today's Reminder

No one in our fellowship is under obligation to anyone else. Let me not adorn myself with a halo for a good deed, for in doing it I have done more for myself than for the person I tried to help. The more light we generate for others, the better we can see ourselves.

Even a word spoken or written in a far-off land may reach me and throw new light on a perplexity of my own.

"How far that little candle throws
his beams. So shines a good deed
in a naughty world."
(Shakespeare: *The Merchant of Venice*)

Heard at a meeting: "I brought my problems to Al-Anon only to learn that I was expected to solve them myself. Al-Anon would provide the light to make it possible.

"This was sharply brought home to me at my second meeting. I told my horror story and ended my recital with a despairing: 'What shall I do?'

"One member spoke up: 'Do the dishes! Take a walk! Read a book! Start somewhere to unhook your mind from confusions, but don't do anything about your problems until you can see them more clearly. You'll change your way of thinking about them and the solutions will come.'

"This, to me, is the Al-Anon program in a nutshell! It kept me so busy that I had no time to wallow in misery any longer."

Today's Reminder

I will not try to make important decisions until I have freed my mind from resentment, self-pity and hopelessness. Then I will be ready.

> "With the serenity I find in Al-Anon
> many of my difficulties solve
> themselves without my help."

Al-Anon has many treasures for me if I am willing to accept them, but none can do more for me than learning really to live in the present. That means being more aware of myself and of small happy things that often dramatize themselves into importance as I observe them with enjoyment.

No matter how grim the situation may be that has troubled all my waking thoughts, there are shining nuggets of pleasantness all around me to distract my mind from its cares. But I must be on the lookout for them so they will not be lost to me!

Today's Reminder

The noted scientist Huxley said it this way: "For every man, the world is as fresh as it was the first day, and as full of untold novelties for *him who has the eyes to see them.*"

This is a constructive and rewarding way to achieve the *detachment* so often mentioned in Al-Anon.

"God make me receptive and aware; restore to me my capacity for wonder."

Setting our goals too high can lead to frustration and worse. The perfectionist, clinging stubbornly to her ideas of what life ought to be, often has difficulty grasping both the *acceptance* and *detachment* elements of the Al-Anon program. She demands too much of herself and of the alcoholic partner.

This compulsive drive for perfection—an unrealistic idealism—can be a neurotic symptom as difficult to deal with as the alcoholic's compulsion to drink. It makes big problems out of little ones, increases our despair when things don't work out as we hope they will and hampers us in coming to terms with life as it is.

Today's Reminder

I will learn to yield a little here and there and accept what I may be impelled to challenge and resist. I will try to achieve a balanced kind of detachment which is not *abandonment of* or *disinterest in* the alcoholic, but a decision not to let myself be touched too deeply by happenings that are essentially unimportant.

> "To adapt ourselves with a quiet
> mind to what is possible and
> attainable, therein lies happiness."

There is an easier way to rid ourselves of painful thoughts and imaginings than by following the philosopher's advice: "Empty your mind. . . ." It is to *replace* worry and distress with something pleasant.

When I do this, I am not running away from my troubles, but clearing my mind of confusion, so I will be better able to make decisions when the time comes to do so.

Constant dwelling on disturbing matters never solves anything; trying to follow the convolutions of a problem only makes me lose all sense of proportion about it.

Today's Reminder

I will turn to simple things: the contemplation of a tree or a cloud; writing a long-deferred letter or making something, perhaps a bird-house, a rag doll or a cake. I will deliberately lose myself in the new preoccupation so that when I come back from it, my thoughts will be freshened and ready to deal clearly with what I have to face.

> "A change of scene, a new interest,
> a creative undertaking—these are
> healing medicine for the troubled."

It is often suggested in Al-Anon that we examine our motives. It isn't easy to ask "Why did I do that?" and conscientiously track the fault to its source. Did I really mean to let those resentful words escape from me—did I intend to hurt? Or was I giving vent to the pressure of a deeper discomfort: guilt, inadequacy or fear? When I looked closely at my reasons, did I believe that what I said or did was justified?

We may justify our actions, but often we only rationalize, or sidestep the truth. As we dig down deep to uncover our motives, we discover how painful it is to admit, even to ourselves, that we are wrong. Al-Anon places a high value on self-honesty; facing up to our faults is the first step toward overcoming them.

Today's Reminder

I am on the way to achieving maturity when I can cheerfully accept the fact that I am not always right. Then new truths can penetrate and open my mind to the helpful influences all around me.

> "Every way of a man is right in
> his own eyes, but God pondereth
> the hearts."
>
> (*Proverbs*)

The subject of the meeting was our Al-Anon slogan *Let Go and Let God.* Three minutes were allotted to each member for comment. Here's what one member said:

"I don't want to shock anybody, but it seems to me some of us take this slogan far too literally. It doesn't mean to just drop all our problems and let God take care of everything. It's up to us to use the intelligence He gave us.

"An odd little thing happened this morning that illustrates the point. I was trying to thread a needle, one of those with a small round eye. I struggled with it, but the point of the thread always slipped by. Automatically I said to myself: 'Relax—let go and let God.' But it still didn't work. Suddenly I got the message: I wasn't using the good sense He gave me. I took one of those long-eye embroidery needles from my pincushion, and quick as a wink it was threaded. A silly little incident, but it can apply to bigger things, too."

Today's Reminder

I won't always look to God to help me when I'm too lazy to do my share of thinking.

"God helps those who help themselves."

Let's think about *group* problems, those disagreements that sometimes happen because
we do not quite understand each other. It is
not surprising that we who have come to Al-
Anon so confused and unhappy, with our
thinking warped by family difficulties, should
find ourselves at odds over some point of procedure or a personal misunderstanding. We all
have different backgrounds, goals, motives,
standards and hopes, and these can come into
conflict when we find it difficult to communicate with each other.

For group problems, as well as for our individual ones, we use that helpful phrase in the
Twelfth Tradition which ends: "ever reminding us to place *principles above personalities.*"

Today's Reminder

Whenever I am tempted to impatience or anger
because someone in my group does not agree with
me, I will remind myself to place *principles above
personalities.* Everything that happens to me as a
person, everything that involves my relations with
my group, can be ironed out by applying Al-Anon
principles. This lifts all discussion far above the
level of personalities and brings about harmoni-
ous solutions.

> "Our common welfare should come
> first; personal progress for the
> greatest number depends on unity."

Today let's think about our *intentions*. The word will suggest to many of us the vast gap between what we *intend* to do, and what we actually do. We *intend* to be kind and tolerant, but some uncontrollable impulse changes our attitude into something we later find ourselves regretting. We *intend* to accomplish so much, but unless we start out with a realistic estimate of what we are capable of doing, we fall far short of our expectations. We *intend* to make a good life for ourselves and our families, but we seem constantly to be deflected from it by others. Or we *permit* the actions of others to prevent us from fulfilling what we hoped to do.

Today's Reminder

My intentions are good. When I do not fulfill them, I am disappointed; I may even be weighed down by a sense of guilt. How can I avoid this? I will try to clarify my intentions, decide what I really mean to do, say and accomplish. This will help me keep my life on a satisfactory, productive course.

"Let me first be sure what I intend
  and the reasons for my choice; this
  will guide my thoughts into constructive
  channels, and keep me from attempting the
  impractical or impossible."

(Celebra Tueli)

"There are some things I absolutely refuse to accept," says a member at a meeting.

This is too often true of someone who suffers from inordinate pride or is unable to admit she is ever wrong.

Before I decide I cannot accept this or that, I had better examine *my* part in the deadlock. Were my expectations unreasonable? Did I demand too much? Am I being confronted with a natural reprisal for my rigid, uncompromising attitude?

If we have hurt someone or demanded too much of them, swift retribution may dismay or infuriate us. Shouldn't we search out the causes and do something to correct them?

Today's Reminder

I may feel ever so justified in "taking a stand" but let me consider whether it was something *I* did that led to the crisis. To remain unyielding may result in disaster I am still less prepared to accept!

> "We are quick enough at perceiving
> and weighing what we suffer from
> others, but we mind not what others
> suffer from us."
>
> *(Thomas A'Kempis)*

There is an old German folk tale in which the Good Fairy brings a child one gift: *the ability to foresee the outcome of everything she does.*

It is a gift we all could use, especially when we give way to despair and decide, at all costs, to free ourselves from a situation that seems unendurable.

If we could visualize the outcome of a move such as breaking up a marriage, for example, we might not be so ready to deprive our children of a parent; we might shrink from the heavy responsibilities we'd have to meet. Above all, we would still have to contend with our own shortcomings, the very ones that may have helped to bring us to the point of desperation.

Today's Reminder

If I want to make a major change which affects other lives as well, let me first consider the possible outcome. Have I really tried to examine and correct my own faults? Is there a way for me to improve my attitude? I will let the great decision wait until I have tried that!

> "The truly wise solution may lie
> in improving myself."

This is the day on which another year closes. It is a good time for a quiet, honest look at my personal progress. Has it been a good year, better than those which went before? Has the day-by-day guidance of the Al-Anon program brought me to a greater realization and acceptance of myself, the unique individual I am?

If I have regrets for errors or omissions, I will dismiss them. The new year which lies before me has no time for futile regrets. I will live just one day at a time, making each one better than the last, as I grow in confidence and faith.

Today's Reminder

Again I resolve to live the coming year one day at a time, easing myself of the burdens of the past and the uncertainties of the future. Whatever may come, I will meet it with a serene mind.

> "And we know that
> all things work together for
> good to them that love God."
>
> (Romans)

PERMISSIONS TO USE
QUOTATIONS

INDEX OF SUBJECTS

You will find this listing of the subjects covered in our book of daily readings a big help, both in planning meetings and for your personal needs.

*   *   *

Acceptance: 32, 47, 76, 86, 129, 135, 358
Advice: 50, 57, 128, 206, 221, 256, 306, 331, 353
Al-Anon: As a fellowship: 201, 203, 304, 323, 344
  As a way of life: 1, 10, 26, 65, 70, 138, 166,
   209, 261, 272, 324, 340, 354
  Meetings: 38, 39, 62, 75, 77, 97, 191, 195,
   230, 329, 353
  Purposes: 75, 88, 127, 128, 134, 329
Alcoholism a disease: 24, 109, 264, 320, 339
Anger: 2, 20, 48, 55, 69, 106, 187, 222, 223, 229,
  238, 241, 255, 293
Anonymity: 18, 66, 230
Arguments: 55, 95, 189, 255, 316
Attitude: 78, 87, 190, 207, 232, 246, 264, 292, 307
Blame: 3, 78, 147, 268, 347
Changing what I can: 17, 25, 58, 70, 72, 92, 99,
  102, 115, 119, 133, 155, 185, 198, 202, 204,
  214, 216, 224, 228, 234, 253, 254, 263, 271

Children: 179, 245
Compassion: 3, 24, 27, 40, 57, 73, 109, 162, 278
Complacency: 197, 237, 262
Controlling: 30, 32, 86, 116, 139, 144, 167, 194, 250, 261, 271, 285, 334
Courage: 84, 119, 157
Courtesy: 48, 159
Crisis: Dealing With: 100, 124
    Creating a: 98, 152
Criticism: 20, 92, 233, 290
Decisions: 13, 28, 137, 243, 303, 365
Despair: 28, 63, 100, 103, 108, 119, 252, 319, 333
Detachment: 3, 7, 29, 51, 54, 83, 98, 131, 150, 151, 183, 196, 225, 250, 259, 267, 285, 286, 308, 321, 357
Divorce: 50, 137, 243, 263, 365
Expectations: 217, 242, 298, 309
Faith: 60, 67, 74, 80, 103, 122, 168, 186, 234, 248, 284, 311, 314
Fear: 52, 73, 84, 193, 328
Forgiveness: 120
Freedom: 74, 129, 224, 269
Frustration: 19, 217, 228, 242, 338, 358
Giving: 10, 53, 153, 160, 287, 288, 304, 348, 355
Gratitude: 6, 8, 46, 64, 126, 253, 283, 319, 345
Guilt: 127, 199, 278
Helping the Alcoholic: 24, 98, 109, 133, 187, 196, 207, 262, 264, 339
Honesty with self: 2, 14, 130, 161, 170, 171, 237, 280, 366
Hope: 94
Humility: 61, 290, 310, 326, 364
Humor: 164
Husbands of alcoholics: 110, 239, 274, 326, 332
Intentions: 363
Joy: 12, 101, 184, 245, 357
Kindness: 20, 299
Love: 5, 113, 160, 165, 257
Martyrdom: 13, 96, 155, 180, 192, 226, 231, 236

Maturity: 198, 214, 360

Meditation: 126, 141, 291, 312, 315, 318

Motives: 101, 112, 130, 137, 146, 155, 202, 270, 296, 360

Newcomers: 53, 81, 94, 142, 206, 277, 289, 349

Open Mind, Keeping an: 49, 97, 200, 275, 317

Patience: 20, 51, 56

Perfection: 358

Prayer: 22, 74, 123, 156, 177, 275, 319

Problem solving: 100, 103, 105, 107, 125, 128, 148, 297, 356

Recovery in Al-Anon: 4, 23, 38, 44, 45, 68, 71, 89, 184, 185, 210, 218, 281, 334, 351

Religion: 122, 258, 330, 346

Resentment: 21, 149, 154, 222, 235, 266

Responsibilty: 195

Sarcasm: 114, 255

Self control: 95, 229, 238

Self-deception: 14, 35, 78, 98, 130, 146, 161, 181, 267, 282

Self esteem: 134, 313

Self knowledge: 2, 14, 21, 115, 117, 136, 146, 156, 170, 171, 247, 249, 265, 280, 296, 350, 364

Self pity: 6, 11, 21, 75, 96, 119, 122, 180, 191, 192, 240, 282, 302

Self respect: 13, 16, 117

Self will: 20, 74, 90, 107, 139, 286, 338

Selfishness: 121

Selflessness: 93

Serenity: 62, 124, 132, 204, 259, 264, 309, 316, 342

Serenity Prayer: 65, 279

Silence: 44, 55, 85, 95, 150, 211, 229, 238

Slips: 73, 147, 207, 239

    In Al-Anon: 84, 337

Sobriety: 8, 15, 31, 37, 56, 64, 73, 118, 188, 225, 227, 262, 283

Sponsorship: 137, 142, 277

Tension relievers: 143, 315, 359
Vengeance: 149
Wisdom: 293, 300, 341
Slogans: In general: 143, 295
  Easy does it: 19, 111, 189, 238, 301
  First things first: 179, 324
  Keep it simple: 143, 205
  Let go and let God: 28, 95, 107, 125, 131, 163,
     220, 294, 361
  Listen and learn: 39, 41, 49, 81, 97, 190, 200,
     255, 273, 317, 343
  Live and let live: 72, 122, 215, 260
  One day at a time: 1, 19, 79, 82, 91, 104, 140,
     182, 193, 212, 219, 244, 302, 328, 352
  Think: 20, 43, 238, 298
Steps: In general: 141
  First: 30, 32, 42, 86, 116, 135, 144, 167, 194
  Second: 33, 145, 168, 265, 300
  Third: 9, 34, 169
  Fourth: 36, 101, 170, 171, 295, 296
  Fifth: 101, 171
  Sixth: 172
  Seventh: 173
  Eighth: 174
  Ninth: 175
  Tenth: 176, 213, 336, 366
  Eleventh: 177, 291, 312, 318
  Twelfth: 153, 178, 195, 335, 343, 348
Traditions: In general: 325, 327
  First: 20, 77, 322
  Second: 276
  Third: 258, 330
  Fourth: 305
  Fifth: 127, 128, 256
  Eighth: 289
  Twelfth: 18, 66, 230, 362

THE TWELVE STEPS

Study of these Steps is essential to progress in the Al-Anon program. The principles they embody are universal, applicable to everyone, whatever his personal creed. In Al-Anon, we strive for an ever-deeper understanding of these Steps, and pray for the wisdom to apply them to our lives.

1. We admitted we were powerless over alcohol—that our lives had become unmanageable.
2. Came to believe that a Power greater than ourselves could restore us to sanity.
3. Made a decision to turn our will and our lives over to the care of God as we understood Him.
4. Made a searching and fearless moral inventory of ourselves.
5. Admitted to God, to ourselves and to another human being the exact nature of our wrongs.
6. Were entirely ready to have God remove all these defects of character.
7. Humbly asked Him to remove our shortcomings.
8. Made a list of all persons we had harmed and became willing to make amends to them all.

9. Made direct amends to such people wherever possible except when to do so would injure them or others.
10. Continued to take personal inventory and when we were wrong, promptly admitted it.
11. Sought through prayer and meditation to improve our conscious contact with God as we understood Him, praying only for knowledge of His will for us and the power to carry that out.
12. Having had a spiritual awakening as the result of these Steps, we tried to carry this message to others, and to practice these principles in all our affairs.

THE TWELVE TRADITIONS

These guidelines are the means of promoting harmony and growth in Al-Anon groups and in the world-wide fellowship of Al-Anon as a whole. Our group experience suggests that our unity depends upon our adherence to these Traditions:

1. Our common welfare should come first; personal progress for the greatest number depends upon unity.

2. For our group purpose there is but one authority—a loving God as He may express Himself in our group conscience. Our leaders are but trusted servants; they do not govern.

3. The relatives of alcoholics, when gathered together for mutual aid, may call themselves an Al-Anon Family Group, provided that, as a group, they have no other affiliation. The only requirement for membership is that there be a problem of alcoholism in a relative or friend.

4. Each group should be autonomous, except in matters affecting another group or Al-Anon or AA as a whole.

5. Each Al-Anon Family Group has but one purpose: to help families of alcoholics. We do this by practicing the Twelve Steps of AA *ourselves*, by encouraging and understanding our alcoholic relatives, and by welcoming and giving comfort to families of alcoholics.

6. Our Al-Anon Family Groups ought never endorse, finance or lend our name to any outside enterprise, lest problems of money, property and prestige divert us from our primary spiritual aim. Although a separate entity, we should always cooperate with Alcoholics Anonymous.

7. Every group ought to be fully self-supporting, declining outside contributions.

8. Al-Anon Twelfth Step work should remain forever nonprofessional, but our service centers may employ special workers.

9. Our groups, as such, ought never be organized; but we may create service boards or committees directly responsible to those they serve.

10. The Al-Anon Family Groups have no opinion on outside issues; hence our name ought never be drawn into public controversy.

11. Our public relations policy is based on attraction rather than promotion; we need always maintain personal anonymity at the level of press, radio, TV and films. We need guard with special care the anonymity of all AA members.

12. Anonymity is the spiritual foundation of all our Traditions, ever reminding us to place principles above personalities.

THE SERENITY PRAYER

This prayer is read at most group meetings and often analyzed in group discussions. It also serves as inspiration to individuals in daily meditation.

> God grant me the serenity
> To accept the things I cannot change,
> Courage to change the things I can,
> And wisdom to know the difference.

THE SLOGANS OF AL-ANON

These slogans are used in the same way as the Serenity Prayer, to seek spiritual guidance in dealing with our conflicts and challenges. Groups use the slogans as subjects for meetings; individuals use them as reminders in times of stress.

Listed below are the slogans which this book discusses. However, many other slogans are popular and have been helpful to Al-Anon members, such as: But for the Grace of God, Keep an Open Mind, and How Important Is It?

> Let Go and Let God
> Easy Does It
> Live and Let Live
> First Things First
> One Day at a Time
> Keep It Simple
> Think
> Listen and Learn